Dec 00'

We think of you often
Always with love
and fond memories
of your smiling faces —
the Longs
Bob, Jeni, Brian & Jessica

L'Chaim!

לחיים

Prayers and Blessings for the Home

Selected and edited by **RABBI DR MICHAEL SHIRE**

ILLUSTRATED WITH ILLUMINATED MANUSCRIPTS
FROM THE BRITISH LIBRARY AND THE BODLEIAN LIBRARY

CHRONICLE

For Anya Sophia Mieze who is our special blessing

*With thanks to Nancy Morris for typing the Hebrew text, to Suzanne
Ophir and Debbie Bloom for proofreading it, and to Victoria Poskitt,
Cathy Fischgrund and Fiona Robertson of Frances Lincoln for their
constant support, skill and encouragement.*

— Michael Shire

First published in Great Britain in 2000 by Frances Lincoln Limited
First published in the United States in 2000 by Chronicle Books LLC

For details about the manuscripts see pp. 74–77

Library of Congress Cataloging-in-Publication Data available.

ISBN 0-8118-2964-2

Printed in Hong Kong

Distributed in Canada by Raincoast Books
9050 Shaughnessy Street
Vancouver, British Columbia V6P 6E5

10 9 8 7 6 5 4 3 2 1

Chronicle Books LLC
85 Second Street
San Francisco, California 94105

www.chroniclebooks.com

CONTENTS

INTRODUCTION

*Prayer cannot bring water to parched fields, nor mend a broken bridge,
nor rebuild a ruined city; but prayer can water an arid soul, mend a
broken heart and rebuild a weakened will* – ABRAHAM JOSHUA HESCHEL

There are a myriad of blessings and prayers for the Jewish home found in liturgies, including the daily and *Shabbat* prayer book (*Siddur*), the *Pesach Haggadah*, the High Holiday and Pilgrim Festivals prayer book (*Machzor*), and prayers for a house of mourning. In this collection, traditional blessings with a gender-free English translation feature alongside newly gathered Hebrew texts from, for example, *The Book of Psalms* and the *Mishnah*, penitential poems from medieval Spain and women's prayers from eighteenth-century Italy. I have tried to give new meaning to the ancient texts by applying them to situations that we face in our lives today.

In Judaism, we mark occasions, ordinary and special, throughout the year with what is called in Hebrew a *brachah*, often translated as 'blessing'. *Brachah* has the same grammatical root as *brecha* which means 'source of water'. Water sustains life and is the source of living things, just as a blessing acknowledges the Creator of life and our reliance on God's providence. When we pause in our activities to recite a *brachah*, we mark a particular moment in our daily lives. The simple phrase 'Blessed are You, Source of all Life' is adapted to every possible occasion and gives us the opportunity to respond to God, life's Source of Blessing.

Indeed, we respond to God with praise and awe through prayer. As we witness the wonders of creation and the achievements of our lives, our prayers and blessings mark special moments and give us the opportunity to acknowledge joy or sorrow, thus bringing God's presence into our lives. From conception to death, prayers and blessings enable us to give thanks, to hope for the things we desire and to respond to the world and the people around us. Prayer does not make us holy; rather, it opens us to holiness.

This book serves as a spiritual guide and connects us with Jewish family life in ages past. The images, which are the visual link with the past, come from beautiful illuminated manuscripts, Ashkenazi and Sephardi in origin, dating from the thirteenth to eighteenth centuries. Rich in hue and ornate in their detail, they portray a wide variety of rituals of Jewish life. They illustrate popular Jewish texts, including the *Pesach Haggadah* and the *Tanach* (the Hebrew Bible).

A rich collection of Jewish art and wisdom, *L'Chaim* reflects the devotion of the Jewish people. Its aim is to fulfill God's purpose in bringing meaning into our lives and providing healing for those around us. I hope it enriches your home as a beautiful reminder of Jewish ceremonial art throughout the ages, and as a guide to the prayers and blessings that shape our faith.

THE CYCLE OF LIFE

To everything is a season and a time for every purpose
under heaven – ECCLESIASTES, 3:1

Birth marks the beginning of the cycle of life, a journey from creation to life everlasting where, in the words of Jose ben Abin, a fourth-century rabbi, two worlds meet with a kiss: this world going out, the future world coming in.

As we move through life, we encounter important moments along the way: personal achievements, *Bar-Mitzvah* and *Bat-Mitzvah*, marriage, anniversaries, the birth of a child, the death of loved ones – all times when, naturally, we contemplate our own existence. We pause and reflect on where we have come from and where we go next. In Judaism, we imbue these moments with special meaning by attaching a prayer or blessing to them. The word 'special' in Hebrew is *kadosh* which also means 'holy'. Through prayer, we usher God's presence into our lives, adding depth and spirituality to these special occasions. They become windows of time to celebrate with our families and our community so that all may share in our blessings. As is written in *The Book of Psalms*: 'So teach us to number our days that we may gain a heart of wisdom.' (*Psalm 90:12*)

All of us have our own journey and it is for us as individuals to decide what events to mark in our lives. As Bachya Ibn Pakuda, an eleventh-century philosopher, has said: 'Days are scrolls, write on them what you want to be remembered.' The prayers and blessings in this section enable us to remember some special moments but, more importantly, they encourage us to mark and give meaning to our days.

FERTILITY AND NEW LIFE

פִּרְיוֹן וְחַיִּים חֲדָשִׁים

For the onset of menstruation:
Blessed are You, Source of all Life, for making me a woman.

בָּרוּךְ אַתָּה יהוה אֱלֹהֵינוּ מֶלֶךְ הָעוֹלָם שֶׁעָשַׂנִי אִשָּׁה:

For attempts to conceive:
God of Creation, if You will look upon the distress of Your servant and remember me and not forsake me, but will give me a child, then I will acknowledge God's presence all the days of my life.
(*I Samuel, 1:11*)

יהוָה צְבָאוֹת אִם־רָאֹה תִרְאֶה בָּעֳנִי אֲמָתֶךָ וּזְכַרְתַּנִי וְלֹא־תִשְׁכַּח אֶת־אֲמָתֶךָ וְנָתַתָּה לַאֲמָתְךָ זֶרַע אֲנָשִׁים וּנְתַתִּיו לַיהוָה כָּל־יְמֵי חַיָּיו

For the onset of pregnancy:
Give thanks to God who is good, whose love is eternal.
(*Psalm 118:1*)

הוֹדוּ לַיהוה כִּי־טוֹב כִּי לְעוֹלָם חַסְדּוֹ:

For the first trimester of pregnancy:
May it be Your will, my God and God of my ancestors, that You grant me the birth of a pure, innocent child. May the child be good, kind and pious to serve as a blessing. Let my child shine as a light to all Israel and Your teaching. Amen, may it be Your will.

יְהִי רָצוֹן מִלְּפָנֶיךָ יהוה אֱלֹהַי וֵאלֹהֵי אֲבוֹתַי שֶׁתְּזַכֵּנִי בְּרַחֲמֶיךָ הָרַבִּים שֶׁהַוָּלָד שֶׁבְּמֵעַי יִהְיֶה בֶּן זָכָר תָּמִים וְשֶׁיִּהְיֶה צַדִּיק חָסִיד קָדוֹשׁ לִבְרָכָה. וְיִהְיֶה מֵאִיר עֵינֵי יִשְׂרָאֵל בְּתוֹרָתֶךָ: אָמֵן. כֵּן יְהִי רָצוֹן.

For the second trimester of pregnancy:
Ruler of the Universe, God of All, the eyes of all look hopefully to You and in time of anxiety seek help from You. Though I am not especially deserving to come before You with my prayer, I am resolved to place myself before You humbly just as You remembered Sarah,

רִבּוֹן הָעוֹלָמִים אֲדוֹן הַצְּבָאוֹת עֵינֵי כֹל אֵלֶיךָ יְשַׂבֵּרוּ וּכְעֵת צָרָה לְךָ יְשַׁוֵּעוּ וְעִם כִּי אֵינִי כְּדַאִית לָבוֹא לְפָנֶיךָ בִּתְפִלָּתִי שַׂמְתִּי פָנַי כַּחַלָּמִישׁ וּבָאתִי לְהַפִּיל תְּחִנָּתִי לְפָנֶיךָ שֶׁכְּשֵׁם שֶׁפָּקַדְתָּ אֶת־שָׂרָה וְנֶעְתַּרְתָּ לְרִבְקָה וְרָאִיתָ בָּעֳנִי לֵאָה וְזָכַרְתָּ אֶת רָחֵל וְשָׁמַעְתָּ

listened to Rebecca, saw Leah's sorrow
and remembered Rachel. You have
heard the voices of all the righteous
women in their pleas to You, so hear my
plea and send a protecting angel to
watch over me and to help me during
this time of my pregnancy.

לְקוֹל הַצַּדְקָנִיּוֹת בְּשַׁוְּעָם אֵלֶיךָ כֵּן
תִּשְׁמַע לְקוֹל שַׁוְעִי וְתִשְׁלַח מַלְאָךְ
הַגּוֹאֵל לְסָמְכֵנִי וּלְעָזְרֵנִי בְּעֵת הֵרָיוֹנִי
זֶה

For the third trimester of pregnancy:
Open up my womb that I may give birth
to this child that is within me at the
proper time, a time of blessing and
deliverance. May the child be vital and
healthy and may I labour to fulfilment.
For in Your hand alone is the key to life
as it is written: God remembered Rachel,
listened to her plea and opened her
womb. Therefore have compassion for
me and my supplication. From the
depths of my heart with my voice, I call
to You. Answer me from Your holy
mountain. Selah.
*The previous three blessings are taken
from an eighteenth-century Italian book
of women's prayers.*

פְּתַח צִירֵי רַחֲמִי לָלֶדֶת הַוָּלָד אֲשֶׁר
בְּקִרְבִּי בְּשָׁעָה רְאוּיָה לָלֶדֶת בְּעֵת
בְּרָכָה וִישׁוּעָה. בְּוָלָד שֶׁל קַיָּמָא שֶׁלֹּא
אִגַּע עַצְמִי לָרִיק וְלֹא אֵלֵד לַבֶּהָלָה
חַס וְשָׁלוֹם. כִּי בְיָדְךָ לְבַד מַפְתֵּחַ שֶׁל
חַיָּה. כְּדִכְתִיב וַיִּזְכּוֹר אֱלֹהִים אֶת
רָחֵל וַיִּשְׁמַע אֵלֶיהָ אֱלֹהִים וַיִּפְתַּח
אֶת־רַחְמָהּ. עַל כֵּן יִכְמְרוּ רַחֲמֶיךָ אֵלָי
תַּחֲנוּנִי וּמִמַּעֲמַקֵּי הַלֵּב קְרָאתִיךָ יְיָ
קוֹלִי אֵלֶיךָ אֶקְרָא וְתַעֲנֵנִי מֵהַר קָדְשְׁךָ
סֶלָה.

For the birth of a child:
This is the day God has made, let us
rejoice and be glad in it.
(*Psalm 118:24*)

זֶה הַיּוֹם עָשָׂה יהוה נָגִילָה וְנִשְׂמְחָה בוֹ

For home birth:
Blessed are You, Source of all Life,
creating man and woman and giving

בָּרוּךְ אַתָּה יהוה אֱלֹהֵינוּ מֶלֶךְ הָעוֹלָם
אֲשֶׁר יָצַר גֶּבֶר וְאִשָּׁה וְנָתַן לָאִשָּׁה

women the privilege of childbirth, creating a new generation that strives to keep Torah and serve God's purpose.

זְכוּת לָלֶדֶת יְלָדִים דּוֹר חָדָשׁ הָעוֹסֵק בִּיצִירָהּ שׁוֹמֵר תּוֹרָה וְעוֹבֵד אֵל אֶחָד

For welcoming a child/grandchild to the home:
Blessed is she (he) who comes in God's name. You are blessed from this house of God.

בָּרוּךְ הַבָּא בְּשֵׁם יהוה בֵּרַכְנוּכֶם מִבֵּית יהוה

For adopting a child:
O God, Bless all of us together in the light of Your presence.

בָּרְכֵנִי אָבִינוּ כֻּלָּנוּ כְּאֶחָד בְּאוֹר פָּנֶיךָ

For miscarriage:
Out of the depths I call You, Eternal One.
O God, listen to my cry.
(Psalm 130:1)

מִמַּעֲמַקִּים קְרָאתִיךָ יהוה אֲדֹנָי שִׁמְעָה בְקוֹלִי

Blessed are You, God, giving strength to the weary.

בָּרוּךְ אַתָּה יהוה הַנּוֹתֵן לַיָּעֵף כֹּחַ

For a nursing mother:
May it be Your will, my God and God of my ancestors, that You provide sustenance for Your servant, this tiny baby, with milk enough for all this baby's needs. Give me the patience and strength to nurse until my baby is satisfied. Let me sleep lightly so that I will hear when my baby cries. Save me from injuring my child in any way. May the words of my mouth and the meditations of my heart be acceptable to You, my rock and my redeemer.
This blessing is taken from an eighteenth-century Italian book of women's prayers.

יְהִי רָצוֹן מִלְּפָנֶיךָ יהוה אֱלֹהַי וֵאלֹהֵי אֲבוֹתַי שֶׁתְּזַמֵּן מָזוֹן עַבְדְּךָ הַתִּינוֹק הַזֶּה בְּרַבּוּי חָלָב דֵי מַחְסוֹרוֹ אֲשֶׁר יֶחְסַר לוֹ. וְשִׂים בְּלִבְבִי הָעֵת שֶׁצָּרִיךְ לְהָנִיקֵהוּ כְּדֵי לָתֵת לוֹ. וְהָקֵל מֵעָלַי הַשֵּׁנָה. וּבְעֵת שִׁיבְכֶּה פְּתַח אָזְנַי כְּדֵי לְשָׁמְעוֹ מִיָּד. וְהַצִּילֵנִי שֶׁלֹּא תִפּוֹל יָדִי עָלָיו בְּעֵת הַשֵּׁנָה וְיָמוּת חַס וְשָׁלוֹם: יִהְיוּ לְרָצוֹן אִמְרֵי־פִי וְהֶגְיוֹן לִבִּי לְפָנֶיךָ יהוה צוּרִי וְגוֹאֲלִי:

In Judaism, there are a series of ceremonies to initiate us into the faith. These ceremonies recognize each person's Covenant with God. They include circumcision, mikveh (immersion in water) and conversion to Judaism.

For Brit Milah (*circumcision of an eight-day-old male*):

Blessed be he who comes in the name of God.

בָּרוּךְ הַבָּא בְּשֵׁם יהוה

God said to Abraham: You shall keep my Covenant: you and your children after you throughout their generations. This is my Covenant which you shall keep, between Me and you and your children after you; every male among you shall be circumcised when he is eight days old.
(*Genesis, 17:9–12*)

וַיֹּאמֶר אֱלֹהִים אֶל־אַבְרָהָם וְאַתָּה אֶת־בְּרִיתִי תִשְׁמֹר אַתָּה וְזַרְעֲךָ אַחֲרֶיךָ לְדֹרֹתָם. זֹאת בְּרִיתִי אֲשֶׁר תִּשְׁמְרוּ בֵּינִי וּבֵינֵיכֶם עָרְלַתְכֶם וְהָיָה לְאוֹת בְּרִית בֵּינִי וּבֵינֵיכֶם וּבֶן־שְׁמֹנַת יָמִים יִמּוֹל לָכֶם כָּל־זָכָר לְדֹרֹתֵיכֶם

The Eternal One your God will circumcise your heart, and the heart of your children, to love the Eternal One your God with all your heart and all your soul, that you may live.
(*Deuteronomy, 30:16*)

וּמָל יהוה אֱלֹהֶיךָ אֶת־לְבָבְךָ וְאֶת־לְבַב זַרְעֶךָ לְאַהֲבָה אֶת־יהוה אֱלֹהֶיךָ בְּכָל־לְבָבְךָ וּבְכָל־נַפְשְׁךָ לְמַעַן חַיֶּיךָ

This is the chair of Elijah. May he be remembered for all that is good.
Blessed are You, Source of all Life, making us holy through Your Commandments and commanding us to carry out circumcision.

זֶה הַכִּסֵּא שֶׁל אֵלִיָּהוּ הַנָּבִיא זָכוּר לַטּוֹב:
בָּרוּךְ אַתָּה יהוה אֱלֹהֵינוּ מֶלֶךְ הָעוֹלָם
אֲשֶׁר קִדְּשָׁנוּ בְּמִצְוֹתָיו וְצִוָּנוּ עַל הַמִּילָה:

The Parents:

Blessed are You, Source of all Life, making us holy through Your Commandments and commanding us to bring our son into the Covenant of our ancestor Abraham.

בָּרוּךְ אַתָּה יהוה אֱלֹהֵינוּ מֶלֶךְ הָעוֹלָם
אֲשֶׁר קִדְּשָׁנוּ בְּמִצְוֹתָיו וְצִוָּנוּ לְהַכְנִיסוֹ
בִּבְרִיתוֹ שֶׁל אַבְרָהָם אָבִינוּ:

Blessed are You, Source of all Life, giving us life, sustaining us and enabling us to reach this special time.

בָּרוּךְ אַתָּה יהוה אֱלֹהֵינוּ מֶלֶךְ הָעוֹלָם
שֶׁהֶחֱיָנוּ וְקִיְּמָנוּ וְהִגִּיעָנוּ לַזְּמַן הַזֶּה:

As he has entered into the Covenant, so may he enter into the world of Torah, marriage and good deeds.

כְּשֵׁם שֶׁנִּכְנַס לַבְּרִית כֵּן יִכָּנֵס לְתוֹרָה
וּלְחֻפָּה וּלְמַעֲשִׂים טוֹבִים:

The Mohel:

Blessed are You, Source of all Life, creating the fruit of the vine.

בָּרוּךְ אַתָּה יהוה אֱלֹהֵינוּ מֶלֶךְ הָעוֹלָם
בּוֹרֵא פְּרִי הַגָּפֶן:

A few drops of wine are given to the child.

May the One who blessed our ancestors Abraham, Isaac and Jacob, Sarah, Rebecca, Rachel and Leah, bless this child, whose name in the House of Israel shall be .... son of ....
May God guard him from all evil, grant him a long life and establish the work of his hands. May his father and mother rejoice in their child and help him to grow and to learn to

מִי שֶׁבֵּרַךְ אֲבוֹתֵינוּ אַבְרָהָם יִצְחָק
וְיַעֲקֹב וְאִמּוֹתֵינוּ שָׂרָה רִבְקָה רָחֵל וְלֵאָה
הוּא יְבָרֵךְ אֶת הַיֶּלֶד הַזֶּה וְיִקָּרֵא שְׁמוֹ
בְּיִשְׂרָאֵל ..... בֶּן .....
הַקָּדוֹשׁ בָּרוּךְ הוּא יִשְׁמְרֵהוּ מִכָּל-רָע וְיִתֵּן
לוֹ חַיִּים אֲרוּכִים וִיכוֹנֵן מַעֲשֵׂה יָדָיו יִשְׂמַח
אָבִיו בְּיוֹצֵא חֲלָצָיו וְתָגֵל אִמּוֹ בִּפְרִי
בִטְנָהּ וְיִזְכּוּ לְגַדְּלוֹ וּלְחַנְּכוֹ כְּדֵי שֶׁיָּבִיא
בְּרָכָה עַל מִשְׁפַּחְתּוֹ וְעַל בֵּית יִשְׂרָאֵל

become a blessing to his family, the family of Israel and all the families of the earth.

May God bless you and help you to see all the blessings in your life. May you feel God's presence near you at all times. May God give you peace and help you to bring peace to your own soul, to your family and to all the world.

For Simchat Bat (*thanksgiving for a baby daughter*):
Blessed are You, Source of all Life, providing kindness and goodness.

May God, who blessed our ancestors Abraham, Isaac and Jacob, Sarah, Rebecca, Rachel and Leah, bless this child, whose name in Israel shall be .... daughter of .... May God guard her from all trouble, grant her a long life and fulfil the work of her hands. May we, her parents, rejoice in our child and help her grow to bring blessings to her family, the family of Israel and all the families of the earth.

Blessed are You, Source of all Life, making us holy through Your Commandments and commanding us to enter our child into the Covenant of Abraham and Sarah.

As she has entered into the Covenant, so may she also enter into the blessings of Torah, marriage and good deeds.

וְעַל כָּל־מִשְׁפְּחֹת הָאֲדָמָה

יְבָרֶכְךָ יהוה וְיִשְׁמְרֶךָ
יָאֵר יהוה פָּנָיו אֵלֶיךָ וִיחֻנֶּךָּ
יִשָּׂא יהוה פָּנָיו אֵלֶיךָ
וְיָשֵׂם לְךָ שָׁלוֹם

בָּרוּךְ אַתָּה יהוה אֱלֹהֵינוּ מֶלֶךְ הָעוֹלָם
הַטּוֹב וְהַמֵּטִיב

מִי שֶׁבֵּרַךְ אֲבוֹתֵינוּ אַבְרָהָם יִצְחָק
וְיַעֲקֹב וְאִמּוֹתֵינוּ שָׂרָה רִבְקָה רָחֵל
וְלֵאָה הוּא יְבָרֵךְ אֶת־הַיַּלְדָּה הַזֹּאת
וְיִקָּרֵא שְׁמָהּ בְּיִשְׂרָאֵל . . . . בַּת . . . .
הַקָּדוֹשׁ בָּרוּךְ הוּא יִשְׁמְרֶהָ מִכָּל־רָע
וְיִתֶּן לָהּ חַיִּים אֲרֻכִּים וִיכוֹנֵן מַעֲשֵׂה
יָדֶיהָ. יִשְׂמַח אָבִיהָ בְּיוֹצֵאת חֲלָצָיו
וְתָגֵל אִמָּהּ בִּפְרִי בִטְנָהּ וְיִזְכּוּ לְגַדְּלָהּ
וּלְחַנְּכָהּ כְּדֵי שֶׁתָּבִיא בְּרָכָה עַל
מִשְׁפַּחְתָּהּ וְעַל בֵּית יִשְׂרָאֵל וְעַל כָּל־
מִשְׁפְּחוֹת הָאֲדָמָה.

בָּרוּךְ אַתָּה יהוה אֱלֹהֵינוּ מֶלֶךְ הָעוֹלָם
אֲשֶׁר קִדְּשָׁנוּ בְּמִצְוֹתָיו וְצִוָּנוּ לְהַכְנִיסָהּ
בִּבְרִיתוֹ שֶׁל אַבְרָהָם וְשָׂרָה

כְּשֵׁם שֶׁנִּכְנְסָה לַבְּרִית כֵּן תִּכָּנֵס
לַתּוֹרָה לְחֻפָּה וּלְמַעֲשִׂים טוֹבִים

May God bless you and help you to see all the blessings in your life. May you feel God's presence near you at all times. May God give you peace and help you to bring peace to your own soul, to your family and to all the world.

יְבָרֶכְךָ יהוה וְיִשְׁמְרֶךָ
יָאֵר יהוה פָּנָיו אֵלֶיךָ וִיחֻנֶּךָּ
יִשָּׂא יהוה פָּנָיו אֵלֶיךָ
וְיָשֵׂם לְךָ שָׁלוֹם:

For attending mikveh (*a pool used for the ritual of immersion in water***):**
Blessed are You, Source of all Life, making us holy through Your Commandments and commanding us to immerse ourselves in water.

בָּרוּךְ אַתָּה יהוה אֱלֹהֵינוּ מֶלֶךְ הָעוֹלָם
אֲשֶׁר קִדְּשָׁנוּ בְּמִצְוֹתָיו וְצִוָּנוּ עַל
הַטְּבִילָה:

On admission to the Jewish faith:
Entreat me not to leave you
Or to turn back from following after you.
For where you will go, I will go.
Where you lodge, I will lodge.
Your people shall be my people,
And your God, my God.
(*Ruth, 1:16*)

וַתֹּאמֶר רוּת אַל־תִּפְגְּעִי־בִי
לְעָזְבֵךְ לָשׁוּב מֵאַחֲרָיִךְ
כִּי אֶל־אֲשֶׁר תֵּלְכִי אֵלֵךְ
וּבַאֲשֶׁר תָּלִינִי אָלִין עַמֵּךְ עַמִּי
וֵאלֹהַיִךְ אֱלֹהָי:

BAR-MITZVAH/BAT-MITZVAH

בַּר/בַּת מִצְוָה

This is the coming-of-age ceremony for adolescents, in which they demonstrate their ability to participate in Jewish community life by reading from the Torah.

For Bar-Mitzvah/Bat-Mitzvah or Kabbalat Torah (*confirmation*):

My God and the God of my ancestors, in truth and sincerity, I lift up my eyes to You on this great and sacred day and say: My childhood days have passed and I take upon myself the responsibilities of a Jew. It is my duty to keep the Commandments and I must answer when called upon for my own actions, for which You hold me responsible. Until now I have been a Jew by birth alone, but today I freely enter Your congregation and before all the world I will revere Your name.

אֱלֹהַי וֵאלֹהֵי אֲבוֹתַי בֶּאֱמֶת וּבְתָמִים אֶשָּׂא
אֵלֶיךָ אֶת־עֵינַי בַּיּוֹם הַגָּדוֹל וְהַקָּדוֹשׁ הַזֶּה
לֵאמֹר הִנֵּה יַלְדוּתִי חָלְפָה הָלְכָה לָהּ
וְאָנֹכִי הָיִיתִי לְאִישׁ עָלַי לִשְׁמוֹר אֶת־כָּל־
חֻקֵּי רְצוֹנֶךָ וְעָלַי לַעֲנוֹת בְּיוֹם פָּקְדָתִי
כַּאֲשֶׁר תִּגְמוֹל לִי כְּפִרְיֵי מַעֲלָלַי מִיּוֹם
הִוָּלְדִי בֶּן יִשְׂרָאֵל אֲנִי אָמְנָם בַּיּוֹם הַזֶּה
בָּאתִי שֵׁנִית בַּקָּהָל לָךְ וְלִפְנֵי כָל־הָעַמִּים
אֶתְפָּאֵר עַל־שִׁמְךָ אֲשֶׁר נִקְרָא עָלֵינוּ

May the One who blessed Abraham, Isaac and Jacob, Sarah, Rebecca, Rachel and Leah bless the Bar-Mitzvah (Bat-Mitzvah) .... who is called to the Torah.

מִי שֶׁבֵּרַךְ אֲבוֹתֵינוּ אַבְרָהָם יִצְחָק וְיַעֲקֹב
וְאִמּוֹתֵינוּ שָׂרָה רִבְקָה רָחֵל וְלֵאָה
הוּא יְבָרֵךְ אֶת־הַבַּר־מִצְוָה/בַּת־הַמִּצְוָה
שֶׁעָלָה/שֶׁעָלְתָה לַתּוֹרָה

For parents to recite:

May you live to see your world fulfilled.
May your destiny be for worlds still to come, and may you trust in generations past and future.
May songs of praise ever be upon your tongue, and your vision be on a straight path before you.
May your eyes shine with the light of Torah, and your face reflect the brightness of the heavens.

(*Talmud Berachot, 17a*)

עוֹלָמֶךָ תִּרְאֶה בְּחַיֶּיךָ
וְאַחֲרִיתְךָ לְחַיֵּי הָעוֹלָם הַבָּא
וְתִקְוָתְךָ לְדוֹר דּוֹרִים
פִּיךָ יְדַבֵּר חָכְמוֹת
וּלְשׁוֹנְךָ יַרְחִישׁ רְנָנוֹת
עַפְעַפֶּיךָ יַיְשִׁירוּ נֶגְדֶּךָ
עֵינֶיךָ יָאִירוּ בִּמְאוֹר תּוֹרָה
וּפָנֶיךָ יַזְהִירוּ כְּזוֹהַר הָרָקִיעַ

For a birthday:

Blessed are You, Source of all Life, giving us life, sustaining us and enabling us to reach this special time.

Five years old is the time to study the Torah, ten years old to study the Mishnah, thirteen years to carry out the Commandments, fifteen to study the Talmud, eighteen for marriage, twenty for a career, thirty for strength, forty for understanding, fifty for giving advice; at sixty comes maturity, at seventy white hairs, at eighty is toughness and ninety is being bent over. Until, at one hundred years, one passes over from this world. May you grow to be one hundred and twenty years.

(*Pirkei Avot, 5:24*)

בָּרוּךְ אַתָּה יהוה אֱלֹהֵינוּ מֶלֶךְ הָעוֹלָם
שֶׁהֶחֱיָנוּ וְקִיְּמָנוּ וְהִגִּיעָנוּ לַזְּמַן הַזֶּה

בֶּן חָמֵשׁ שָׁנִים לַמִּקְרָא בֶּן עֶשֶׂר שָׁנִים
לַמִּשְׁנָה בֶּן שְׁלֹשׁ עֶשְׂרֵה לַמִּצְוֹת
בֶּן חֲמֵשׁ עֶשְׂרֵה לַגְּמָרָא בֶּן שְׁמוֹנֶה
עֶשְׂרֵה לַחֻפָּה בֶּן עֶשְׂרִים לִרְדּוֹף
בֶּן שְׁלוֹשִׁים לַכֹּחַ בֶּן אַרְבָּעִים לַבִּינָה בֶּן
חֲמִשִּׁים לָעֵצָה בֶּן שִׁשִּׁים לַזִּקְנָה בֶּן
שִׁבְעִים לַשֵּׂיבָה בֶּן שְׁמוֹנִים לַגְּבוּרָה בֶּן
תִּשְׁעִים לָשׁוּחַ בֶּן מֵאָה כְּאִלּוּ מֵת וְעָבַר
וּבָטֵל מִן הָעוֹלָם עַד מֵאָה וְעֶשְׂרִים

Read the psalm that corresponds to your age.

For leaving home:

Go forth from your country, from your birth place, from your parents' house to a place that I shall lead you to. I will make you great and I shall bless you. I will make your name great and therefore you shall be a blessing to others. I shall bless those that bless you and afflict those who afflict you. Because through you, all the families of the earth shall be blessed.

(*Genesis, 12:1–3*)

לֶךְ־לְךָ מֵאַרְצְךָ וּמִמּוֹלַדְתְּךָ וּמִבֵּית
אָבִיךָ אֶל־הָאָרֶץ אֲשֶׁר אַרְאֶךָּ
וְאֶעֶשְׂךָ לְגוֹי גָּדוֹל וַאֲבָרֶכְךָ וַאֲגַדְּלָה שְׁמֶךָ
וֶהְיֵה בְּרָכָה:
וַאֲבָרֲכָה מְבָרְכֶיךָ וּמְקַלֶּלְךָ אָאֹר וְנִבְרְכוּ
בְךָ כֹּל מִשְׁפְּחֹת הָאֲדָמָה

For doing something for the first time this year:

Blessed are You, Source of all Life, giving us life, sustaining us and enabling us to reach this special time.

בָּרוּךְ אַתָּה יהוה אֱלֹהֵינוּ מֶלֶךְ הָעוֹלָם
שֶׁהֶחֱיָנוּ וְקִיְּמָנוּ וְהִגִּיעָנוּ לַזְּמַן הַזֶּה:

For the beginning of study:

Blessed are You, Source of all Life, making us holy through Your Commandments and commanding us to immerse ourselves in study.

בָּרוּךְ אַתָּה יהוה אֱלֹהֵינוּ מֶלֶךְ הָעוֹלָם אֲשֶׁר קִדְּשָׁנוּ בְּמִצְוֹתָיו וְצִוָּנוּ לַעֲסוֹק בְּדִבְרֵי תוֹרָה

For the end of study:

For all Israel and their rabbis and all their students and all the students of the students and all those who devote themselves to the study of Torah, in this place and in every place, let there be for us and for them, great peace and blessing, love and compassion, a life of accomplishment and plenty, and fulfilment from God above. Amen.

עַל יִשְׂרָאֵל וְעַל רַבָּנָן וְעַל תַּלְמִידֵיהוֹן וְעַל כָּל תַּלְמִידֵי תַלְמִידֵיהוֹן וְעַל כָּל מָאן דְּעָסְקִין בְּאוֹרַיְתָא דִּי בְּאַתְרָא הָדֵין וְדִי בְכָל אֲתַר וַאֲתַר יְהֵא לְהוֹן וּלְכוֹן שְׁלָמָא רַבָּא חִנָּא וְחִסְדָּא וְרַחֲמִין וְחַיִּין אֲרִיכִין וּמְזוֹנָא רְוִיחָא וּפֻרְקָנָא מִן קֳדָם אֲבוּהוֹן דִּי בִשְׁמַיָּא וְאִמְרוּ אָמֵן

For retirement:

How pleasing is the wisdom of the experienced, the thinking and the advice of the honoured ones.

(*Ben Sira, 25:5*)

מַה-נָּאָה חָכְמָה לִזְקֵנִים וְלִנְכְבָּדִים מַחֲשָׁבָה וְעֵצָה

The righteous shall flourish like a palm tree and grow tall like a cedar in Lebanon that is planted in the house of God. They shall flourish in the courtyards of our God, bearing new fruit in old age, still fresh and still green, proclaiming that God is upright, my rock, in whom there is no wrong.

(*Psalm 92:12–15*)

צַדִּיק כַּתָּמָר יִפְרָח כְּאֶרֶז בַּלְּבָנוֹן יִשְׂגֶּה: שְׁתוּלִים בְּבֵית יהוה בְּחַצְרוֹת אֱלֹהֵינוּ יַפְרִיחוּ: עוֹד יְנוּבוּן בְּשֵׂיבָה דְּשֵׁנִים וְרַעֲנַנִּים יִהְיוּ: לְהַגִּיד כִּי-יָשָׁר יהוה צוּרִי וְלֹא-עַוְלָתָה בּוֹ:

For engagement:
I will betroth you to me forever.
I will betroth you to me in righteousness and
justice, in love and compassion.
I will betroth you to me in faithfulness and
so you will know God.
(*Hosea, 2:21*)

וְאֵרַשְׂתִּיךְ לִי לְעוֹלָם
וְאֵרַשְׂתִּיךְ לִי בְּצֶדֶק וּבְמִשְׁפָּט וּבְחֶסֶד
וּבְרַחֲמִים
וְאֵרַשְׂתִּיךְ לִי בֶּאֱמוּנָה וְיָדַעַתְּ אֶת יהוה

Blessed are You, Source of all Life, creating
the fruit of the vine.

בָּרוּךְ אַתָּה יהוה אֱלֹהֵינוּ מֶלֶךְ הָעוֹלָם
בּוֹרֵא פְּרִי הַגָּפֶן:

Blessed are You, Source of all Life, making us
holy through Your Commandments and
guiding us in our relationships towards
commitment and marriage under a chuppah.
Blessed are You, Source of all Life, who
makes Your people holy through the sanctity
of marriage.

בָּרוּךְ אַתָּה יהוה אֱלֹהֵינוּ מֶלֶךְ הָעוֹלָם
אֲשֶׁר קִדְּשָׁנוּ בְּמִצְוֹתָיו וְצִוָּנוּ עַל הָעֲרָיוֹת
וְאָסַר לָנוּ אֶת הָאֲרוּסוֹת וְהִתִּיר לָנוּ
אֶת הַנְּשׂוּאוֹת לָנוּ עַל יְדֵי חֻפָּה וְקִדּוּשִׁין
בָּרוּךְ אַתָּה יהוה מְקַדֵּשׁ עַמּוֹ יִשְׂרָאֵל
עַל יְדֵי חֻפָּה וְקִדּוּשִׁין:

Set me as a seal upon your heart,
Like the seal upon your hand;
For love is as strong as death,
It is the flame of God.
(*Song of Songs, 8:6*)

שִׂימֵנִי כַחוֹתָם עַל־לִבֶּךָ
כַּחוֹתָם עַל־זְרוֹעֶךָ כִּי־עַזָּה
כַמָּוֶת אַהֲבָה קָשָׁה
כִשְׁאוֹל קִנְאָה רְשָׁפֶיהָ
רִשְׁפֵּי אֵשׁ שַׁלְהֶבֶתְיָה

The Seven Wedding Blessings:
Blessed are You, Source of all Life, creating
the fruit of the vine.

בָּרוּךְ אַתָּה יהוה אֱלֹהֵינוּ מֶלֶךְ הָעוֹלָם
בּוֹרֵא פְּרִי הַגָּפֶן:

Blessed are You, Source of all Life, every act
of Your creation makes us aware of Your
presence.

בָּרוּךְ אַתָּה יהוה אֱלֹהֵינוּ מֶלֶךְ הָעוֹלָם
שֶׁהַכֹּל בָּרָא לִכְבוֹדוֹ:

Blessed are You, Source of all Life, calling
humanity into being.

בָּרוּךְ אַתָּה יהוה אֱלֹהֵינוּ מֶלֶךְ הָעוֹלָם
יוֹצֵר הָאָדָם:

Blessed are You, Source of all Life, fashioning us in Your image and giving us, through marriage, the opportunity for commitment in life together.

Zion, once faced with hopelessness, shall now rejoice as her children gather with joy in the midst. Blessed are You, Source of all Life, causing Zion to rejoice in her children.

May these two, lovers and friends, find bliss as did the first human couple in the Garden of Eden. Blessed are You for the happiness of the groom and the bride.

Blessed are You, Source of all Life, creating exultation and joy, groom and bride, merriment and song, love and closeness, fulfilment and friendship. Soon may the streets of Jerusalem, as everywhere, reverberate with joyous sounds: the voice of groom and bride, of happy couples emerging from the chuppah with their friends in celebration. Blessed are You, for the happiness which the groom and bride find in each other.

For a wedding anniversary:
My beloved is mine and I am his.
(*Song of Songs, 2:16*)

The voice of my beloved!
He comes leaping over mountains, skipping over hills.
My beloved is like a gazelle or like a young stag.
There he stands behind our wall, gazing through the window, peering through the lattice.

בָּרוּךְ אַתָּה יהוה אֱלֹהֵינוּ מֶלֶךְ הָעוֹלָם אֲשֶׁר יָצַר אֶת הָאָדָם בְּצַלְמוֹ. בְּצֶלֶם דְּמוּת תַּבְנִיתוֹ. וְהִתְקִין לוֹ מִמֶּנּוּ בִּנְיַן עֲדֵי עַד. בָּרוּךְ אַתָּה יהוה יוֹצֵר הָאָדָם

שׂוֹשׂ תָּשִׂישׂ וְתָגֵל הָעֲקָרָה בְּקִבּוּץ בָּנֶיהָ לְתוֹכָהּ בְּשִׂמְחָה. בָּרוּךְ אַתָּה יהוה מְשַׂמֵּחַ צִיּוֹן בְּבָנֶיהָ:

שַׂמֵּחַ תְּשַׂמַּח רֵעִים הָאֲהוּבִים. כְּשַׂמֵּחֲךָ יְצִירְךָ בְּגַן עֵדֶן מִקֶּדֶם. בָּרוּךְ אַתָּה יהוה מְשַׂמֵּחַ חָתָן וְכַלָּה:

בָּרוּךְ אַתָּה יהוה אֱלֹהֵינוּ מֶלֶךְ הָעוֹלָם. אֲשֶׁר בָּרָא שָׂשׂוֹן וְשִׂמְחָה חָתָן וְכַלָּה. גִּילָה רִנָּה דִּיצָה וְחֶדְוָה. אַהֲבָה וְאַחֲוָה וְשָׁלוֹם וְרֵעוּת. מְהֵרָה יהוה אֱלֹהֵינוּ יִשָּׁמַע בְּעָרֵי יְהוּדָה וּבְחֻצוֹת יְרוּשָׁלַיִם קוֹל שָׂשׂוֹן וְקוֹל שִׂמְחָה. קוֹל חָתָן וְקוֹל כַּלָּה. קוֹל מִצְהֲלוֹת חֲתָנִים מֵחֻפָּתָם וּנְעָרִים מִמִּשְׁתֵּה נְגִינָתָם. בָּרוּךְ אַתָּה יהוה מְשַׂמֵּחַ חָתָן עִם הַכַּלָּה:

דּוֹדִי לִי וַאֲנִי לוֹ

קוֹל דּוֹדִי הִנֵּה־זֶה בָּא מְדַלֵּג עַל־הֶהָרִים מְקַפֵּץ עַל־הַגְּבָעוֹת. דּוֹמֶה דוֹדִי לִצְבִי אוֹ לְעֹפֶר הָאַיָּלִים הִנֵּה־זֶה עוֹמֵד אַחַר כָּתְלֵנוּ מַשְׁגִּיחַ מִן־הַחַלֹּנוֹת מֵצִיץ מִן־הַחֲרַכִּים

My beloved speaks to me, saying: Rise up, my love, my fair one and come away.

For, lo, the winter is past, the rain is over and gone.

The flowers appear on the earth, the time of singing has come, and the voice of the turtle dove is heard in our land.

The fig tree puts forth green figs and the vines with tender grapes give off sweet fragrance.

Arise, my love, my fair one, and come away.
(*Song of Songs, 2:8–13*)

עָנָה דוֹדִי וְאָמַר לִי
קוּמִי לָךְ רַעְיָתִי יָפָתִי וּלְכִי־לָךְ
כִּי־הִנֵּה הַסְּתָו עָבָר הַגֶּשֶׁם חָלַף הָלַךְ
לוֹ: הַנִּצָּנִים נִרְאוּ בָאָרֶץ
עֵת הַזָּמִיר הִגִּיעַ
וְקוֹל הַתּוֹר נִשְׁמַע בְּאַרְצֵנוּ: הַתְּאֵנָה
חָנְטָה פַגֶּיהָ וְהַגְּפָנִים סְמָדַר נָתְנוּ רֵיחַ
קוּמִי לָכִי רַעְיָתִי יָפָתִי וּלְכִי־לָךְ:

For a silver/golden wedding anniversary:
Blessed are You, Source of all Life, giving us life, sustaining us and enabling us to reach this special time.

Blessed are You, Source of all Life, who causes the bridegroom to rejoice with the bride.

בָּרוּךְ אַתָּה יהרה אֱלֹהֵינוּ מֶלֶךְ הָעוֹלָם
שֶׁהֶחֱיָנוּ וְקִיְּמָנוּ וְהִגִּיעָנוּ לַזְּמַן הַזֶּה:

בָּרוּךְ אַתָּה יהוה מְשַׂמֵּחַ חָתָן עִם הַכַּלָּה:

DEATH AND MOURNING

מָוֶת וַאֲבֵילוּת

In Judaism, the rituals around death and mourning reflect the emotional turmoil of mourners, from the funeral to yahrzeit, *the commitment each year to remember loved ones.*

On a deathbed:

Eternal God, You reign, You have reigned,
You will reign for ever.
Praised is Your glorious reign for ever.
The Eternal One is Your God.
Hear O Israel, the Eternal One is Your God,
the Eternal is One.

יהוה מֶלֶךְ. יהוה מָלָךְ.
יהוה יִמְלוֹךְ לְעֹלָם וָעֶד:
בָּרוּךְ שֵׁם כְּבוֹד מַלְכוּתוֹ לְעוֹלָם וָעֶד:
יהוה הוּא הָאֱלֹהִים:
שְׁמַע יִשְׂרָאֵל יהוה אֱלֹהֵינוּ יהוה אֶחָד:

Blessed be the true judge.

בָּרוּךְ דַּיָּן הָאֱמֶת

For a yahrzeit (*anniversary of a death*):

God, full of compassion, whose presence hovers over us, grant perfect rest beneath the shelter of Your presence with the holy and pure who shine as the lights of heaven to ...., who has gone to her (his) everlasting home. God of mercy, spread over her (him) the shelter of Your wings forever and bind her (his) soul in the bond of Eternal Life. It is God who is her (his) heritage. May she (he) be at peace in her (his) place of rest. Amen.

אֵל מָלֵא רַחֲמִים שׁוֹכֵן בַּמְּרוֹמִים הַמְצָא
מְנוּחָה נְכוֹנָה עַל כַּנְפֵי הַשְּׁכִינָה בְּמַעֲלוֹת
קְדוֹשִׁים וּטְהוֹרִים כְּזֹהַר הָרָקִיעַ
מַזְהִירִים אֶת נִשְׁמַת . . . שֶׁהָלַךְ\שֶׁהָלְכָה
לְעוֹלָמוֹ\לְעוֹלָמָהּ: אָנָּא בַּעַל הָרַחֲמִים
הַסְתִּירֵהוּ\הַסְתִּירֶהָ בְּסֵתֶר כְּנָפֶיךָ
לְעוֹלָמִים וּצְרוֹר בִּצְרוֹר הַחַיִּים אֶת
נִשְׁמָתוֹ\וְנִשְׁמָתָהּ. יהוה הוּא נַחֲלָתוֹ\
נַחֲלָתָהּ. וְיָנוּחַ\וְתָנוּחַ בְּשָׁלוֹם עַל מִשְׁכָּבוֹ\
מִשְׁכָּבָהּ וְנֹאמַר אָמֵן:

Light the yahrzeit candle

The memory of the righteous is a blessing.

זֵכֶר צַדִּיק לִבְרָכָה:

For Kaddish (*the mourner's prayer*):

Let God's name be made great and holy in the world that was created as God willed. May God complete the work of creation in your own lifetime, in your days and in the days of all the House of Israel, quickly and soon. Amen.

May God's great name be blessed, for ever and ever.

May God's name be blessed, praised, glorified, revered, held in awe, acclaimed and revered though it is higher than all the blessings, songs, praises and consolations that can be spoken in this world.

May Heaven grant a universal peace and life for us and for all Israel. Amen.

May the One who created harmony above make peace for us, for all Israel and for all who dwell on earth. Amen.

יִתְגַּדַּל וְיִתְקַדַּשׁ שְׁמֵהּ רַבָּא בְּעָלְמָא דִּי בְרָא כִרְעוּתֵיהּ וְיַמְלִיךְ מַלְכוּתֵהּ בְּחַיֵּיכוֹן וּבְיוֹמֵיכוֹן וּבְחַיֵּי דִי־כָל בֵּית יִשְׂרָאֵל בַּעֲגָלָא וּבִזְמַן קָרִיב. וְאִמְרוּ אָמֵן: יְהֵא שְׁמֵהּ רַבָּא מְבָרַךְ לְעָלַם וּלְעָלְמֵי עָלְמַיָּא. יִתְבָּרַךְ וְיִשְׁתַּבַּח וְיִתְפָּאַר וְיִתְרוֹמַם וְיִתְנַשֵּׂא וְיִתְהַדָּר וְיִתְעַלֶּה וְיִתְהַלָּל שְׁמֵהּ דִּי־קֻדְשָׁא. בְּרִיךְ הוּא. לְעֵלָּא מִן־כָּל־בִּרְכָתָא וְשִׁירָתָא תֻּשְׁבְּחָתָא וְנֶחֱמָתָא דִּי־אֲמִירָן בְּעָלְמָא. וְאִמְרוּ אָמֵן: יְהֵא שְׁלָמָא רַבָּא מִן־שְׁמַיָּא וְחַיִּים עָלֵינוּ וְעַל־כָּל־יִשְׂרָאֵל. וְאִמְרוּ אָמֵן: עֹשֶׂה שָׁלוֹם בִּמְרוֹמָיו הוּא יַעֲשֶׂה שָׁלוֹם עָלֵינוּ וְעַל כָּל־יִשְׂרָאֵל וְעַל כָּל־בְּנֵי־אָדָם. וְאִמְרוּ אָמֵן:

Greeting a mourner:

May God comfort you amongst all others, mourners in Zion and Jerusalem.

הַמָּקוֹם יְנַחֵם אֶתְכֶם בְּתוֹךְ שְׁאָר אֲבֵלֵי צִיּוֹן וִירוּשָׁלָיִם:

THE JEWISH CALENDAR

These are the fixed times, the sacred occasions of the year, which you shall celebrate each at its appointed time — LEVITICUS, 23:4

Gazing at the moon is an age-old Jewish pastime. We follow its waxing and waning to mark the course of the seasons and our Jewish festivals. In the Hebrew calendar each month begins with the appearance of the new moon, a time of joy.

In ancient times, the new moon ceremony was a significant ritual, especially for women, because it celebrates the monthly cycle of fertility. *Rosh Chodesh* is a renewal of God's presence each month through the female aspect of God, the *Shechinah*. The full moon also heralds special times of the year. The ancient biblical festivals of *Sukkot, Pesach* and *Shavuot* all commence on the full moon, an abundant and auspicious time for celebration and worship.

Just as months are determined by the travels of the moon, years depend on the earth's rotation around the sun. *Shabbat* and the festivals begin and end at sunset. As the foremost Jewish celebration, *Shabbat* sanctifies the Jewish home, replacing the ancient biblical rituals of the Temple in Jerusalem. Today it is the mainstay of Jewish family life, offering a weekly respite from work, and a time to be rather than to have. Ahad Ha'am, the famous nineteenth-century Jewish essayist, poignantly remarked: 'More than Israel has kept the *Shabbat*, the *Shabbat* has kept Israel.'

Whether during *Shabbat* or a festival, it is the ceremonies and rituals in the home that create the sense of occasion. *Shabbat* food, family *sedarim*, home-made *Sukkot* and *Chanukah* lights are the basis for a spiritual life. In our home, it is the custom on Friday night for all present to reflect on the week and offer blessings to each other. The home becomes the *Mikdash Me'at*, a small sanctuary that restores us to a state of rest and love.

The Jewish calendar differs from the secular calendar in that it combines a monthly lunar cycle and an annual solar cycle. Each Jewish month has its own distinctive name, which overlaps with corresponding secular months, beginning with Tishri in September/October.

For Rosh Chodesh (*the celebration to mark a new Jewish month***):**

May it be Your will, Our God and God of our ancestors, that this new month be renewed for goodness and blessing. Give us a long life, a life filled with peace, a life filled with goodness, a life filled with blessing, a life in which there is awe of God and a fear of wrongdoing, a life in which there is no shame or regret, a life full of love of the Torah, a life in which the desires of our hearts may be filled with goodness. Amen. Rosh Chodesh .... will be on ....

May it come to us and all Israel for good. May the Holy One bring us and all the House of Israel a new month of life and peace, happiness and joy, sustenance and comfort. Amen.

יְהִי רָצוֹן מִלְּפָנֶיךָ יהוה אֱלֹהֵינוּ וֵאלֹהֵי אֲבוֹתֵינוּ שֶׁתְּחַדֵּשׁ עָלֵינוּ אֶת־הַחֹדֶשׁ הַזֶּה לְטוֹבָה וְלִבְרָכָה. וְתִתֶּן־לָנוּ חַיִּים אֲרֻכִּים חַיִּים שֶׁל־שָׁלוֹם חַיִּים שֶׁל־טוֹבָה חַיִּים שֶׁל־בְּרָכָה. חַיִּים שֶׁיֵּשׁ בָּהֶם יִרְאַת שָׁמַיִם וְיִרְאַת חֵטְא חַיִּים שֶׁאֵין בָּהֶם בּוּשָׁה וּכְלִמָּה. חַיִּים שֶׁל אַהֲבַת תּוֹרָה. חַיִּים שֶׁיִּמָּלְאוּ מִשְׁאֲלוֹת לִבֵּנוּ לְטוֹבָה. אָמֵן: רֹאשׁ חֹדֶשׁ . . . . . יִהְיֶה בְּיוֹם . . . הַבָּא עָלֵינוּ וְעַל כָּל־יִשְׂרָאֵל לְטוֹבָה: יְחַדְּשֵׁהוּ הַקָּדוֹשׁ בָּרוּךְ הוּא עָלֵינוּ וְעַל כָּל־ עַמּוֹ בֵּית יִשְׂרָאֵל לְחַיִּים וּלְשָׁלוֹם לְשָׂשׂוֹן וּלְשִׂמְחָה. לִישׁוּעָה וּלְנֶחָמָה. וְנֹאמַר אָמֵן:

Birkat Halevana (*a blessing to mark the appearance of a new moon*):

Recited in the open air when the new moon is visible.

Blessed are You, Source of all Life, creating the heavens according to Your word and all the heavenly bodies by Your spirit. You have given them fixed laws and time so that they will not change from their set purpose. They are happy and joyful to do the will of their Creator, whose creation is complete. God orders the moon to renew itself as a wondrous crown over God's creatures. All will be renewed in time and thereby praise the Creator for the magnificent natural world. Blessed are You, renewing the months.

בָּרוּךְ אַתָּה יהוה אֱלֹהֵינוּ מֶלֶךְ הָעוֹלָם אֲשֶׁר בְּמַאֲמָרוֹ בָּרָא שְׁחָקִים וּבְרוּחַ פִּיו כָּל צְבָאָם. חֹק וּזְמַן נָתַן לָהֶם שֶׁלֹּא יְשַׁנּוּ אֶת תַּפְקִידָם. שָׂשִׂים וּשְׂמֵחִים לַעֲשׂוֹת רְצוֹן קוֹנָם פּוֹעֵל אֱמֶת שֶׁפְּעֻלָּתוֹ אֱמֶת וְלַלְּבָנָה אָמַר שֶׁתִּתְחַדֵּשׁ עֲטֶרֶת תִּפְאֶרֶת לַעֲמוּסֵי בָטֶן שֶׁהֵם עֲתִידִים לְהִתְחַדֵּשׁ כְּמוֹתָהּ וּלְפָאֵר לְיוֹצְרָם עַל שֵׁם כְּבוֹד מַלְכוּתוֹ. בָּרוּךְ אַתָּה יהוה מְחַדֵּשׁ חֳדָשִׁים:

For Tishri (*Libra*):
Sing to God a new song, sing to God all the earth.
Sing to God, bless God's name, declare God's sustenance every day.
God will judge the world with righteousness and its people with compassion.
(*Psalm 96:1–2, 13*)

שִׁירוּ לַיהוה שִׁיר חָדָשׁ שִׁירוּ לַיהוה כָּל־הָאָרֶץ:
שִׁירוּ לַיהוה בָּרְכוּ שְׁמוֹ בַּשְּׂרוּ מִיּוֹם־לְיוֹם יְשׁוּעָתוֹ:
סַפְּרוּ בַגּוֹיִם כְּבוֹדוֹ בְּכָל־הָעַמִּים נִפְלְאוֹתָיו: לִפְנֵי יהוה
כִּי בָא כִּי בָא לִשְׁפֹּט הָאָרֶץ יִשְׁפֹּט תֵּבֵל בְּצֶדֶק וְעַמִּים בֶּאֱמוּנָתוֹ:

For Cheshvan (*Scorpio*):
So teach us to count our days that we may gain a heart of wisdom.
(*Psalm 90:12*)

לִמְנוֹת יָמֵינוּ כֵּן הוֹדַע וְנָבִא לְבַב חָכְמָה:

For Kislev (*Sagittarius*):
Blessed is the match consumed in kindling flame.

אַשְׁרֵי הַגַּפְרוּר שֶׁנִּשְׂרַף וְהִצִּית לֶהָבוֹת:

Blessed is the flame that burns in the heart's secret places.
Blessed is the heart with the strength to stop its beating for integrity's sake.
Blessed is the match consumed in kindling flame.

(*Hannah Senesh*)

אַשְׁרֵי הַלְהָבָה שֶׁבָּעֲרָה בְּסִתְרֵי לְבָבוֹת
אַשְׁרֵי הַלְּבָבוֹת שֶׁיָּדְעוּ לַחְדֹּל בְּכָבוֹד
אַשְׁרֵי הַגַּפְרוּר שֶׁנִּשְׂרַף וְהִצִּית לְהָבוֹת

For Tevet (*Capricorn*):

At our gates are all manner of choice fruits, new and old, which I have stored away for you.

(*Song of Songs, 7:14*)

וְעַל־פְּתָחֵינוּ כָּל־מְגָדִים חֲדָשִׁים גַּם־
יְשָׁנִים דּוֹדִי צָפַנְתִּי לָךְ:

For Shevat (*Aquarius*):

And God said: Let the earth bring forth vegetation, seed-bearing plants and fruit trees of every kind. And God saw that it was good.

(*Genesis, 1:11, 12*)

וַיֹּאמֶר אֱלֹהִים תַּדְשֵׁא הָאָרֶץ דֶּשֶׁא עֵשֶׂב
מַזְרִיעַ זֶרַע עֵץ פְּרִי עֹשֶׂה פְּרִי לְמִינוֹ
אֲשֶׁר זַרְעוֹ־בוֹ עַל־הָאָרֶץ וַיְהִי־כֵן: וַיַּרְא
אֱלֹהִים כִּי־טוֹב:

For Adar (*Pisces*):

When the month of Adar begins, rejoicing is increased.

(*Mishnah Taanit, 29a*)

מִשֶּׁנִּכְנַס אֲדָר מַרְבִּין בְּשִׂמְחָה:

For Nisan (*Aries*):

When Israel came out of Egypt, the house of Jacob from a foreign land, then Judah was made holy and Israel served God. The sea saw it and split in two, the Jordan turned back, the mountains danced like rams, the hills like young lambs.

(*Psalm 114:1–4*)

בְּצֵאת יִשְׂרָאֵל מִמִּצְרָיִם בֵּית יַעֲקֹב מֵעַם
לֹעֵז: הָיְתָה יְהוּדָה לְקָדְשׁוֹ יִשְׂרָאֵל
מַמְשְׁלוֹתָיו: הַיָּם רָאָה וַיָּנֹס הַיַּרְדֵּן יִסֹּב
לְאָחוֹר: הֶהָרִים רָקְדוּ כְאֵילִים גְּבָעוֹת
כִּבְנֵי־צֹאן:

For Iyyar (*Taurus*):

If I forget you, O Jerusalem, let my right hand wither. Let my tongue cleave to

אִם־אֶשְׁכָּחֵךְ יְרוּשָׁלַ͏ִם תִּשְׁכַּח יְמִינִי
תִּדְבַּק־לְשׁוֹנִי לְחִכִּי אִם־לֹא אֶזְכְּרֵכִי

the roof of my mouth if I do not remember you, if I do not set Jerusalem above my highest joy.
(*Psalm 137:5–6*)

אִם־לֹא אַעֲלֶה אֶת־יְרוּשָׁלַם עַל רֹאשׁ שִׂמְחָתִי:

For Sivan (*Gemini*):
The Torah is a tree of life to those who hold fast to it and all who cling to it are happy. Its ways are ways of pleasantness and all its paths are peace.
(*Proverbs, 3:17, 18*)

עֵץ־חַיִּים הִיא לַמַּחֲזִיקִים בָּהּ וְתֹמְכֶיהָ מְאֻשָּׁר: דְּרָכֶיהָ דַרְכֵי־נֹעַם וְכָל־נְתִיבוֹתֶיהָ שָׁלוֹם:

For Tammuz (*Cancer*):
Comfort my people, comfort them, says our God. Speak comfortingly to Jerusalem and say to her that her service is ended and her sin is pardoned. Every valley shall be raised up and every mountain and hill made low, the crooked shall be straightened and the rough places smoothed.
(*Isaiah, 40:1–4*)

נַחֲמוּ נַחֲמוּ עַמִּי יֹאמַר אֱלֹהֵיכֶם: דַּבְּרוּ עַל־לֵב יְרוּשָׁלַם וְקִרְאוּ אֵלֶיהָ כִּי מָלְאָה צְבָאָהּ כִּי נִרְצָה עֲוֺנָהּ כִּי לָקְחָה מִיַּד יהוה כִּפְלַיִם בְּכָל־חַטֹּאתֶיהָ: קוֹל קוֹרֵא בַּמִּדְבָּר פַּנּוּ דֶּרֶךְ יהוה יַשְּׁרוּ בָּעֲרָבָה מְסִלָּה לֵאלֹהֵינוּ: כָּל־גֶּיא יִנָּשֵׂא וְכָל־הַר וְגִבְעָה יִשְׁפָּלוּ וְהָיָה הֶעָקֹב לְמִישׁוֹר וְהָרְכָסִים לִבְקְעָה:

For Av (*Leo*):
How solitary sits the city that was once full of people. She has become like a widow, she who was great among the nations. Cause us to turn to You, O God, and we shall return. Renew our days as in the past.
(*Lamentations, 1:1, 5:21*)

אֵיכָה יָשְׁבָה בָדָד הָעִיר רַבָּתִי עָם הָיְתָה כְּאַלְמָנָה רַבָּתִי בַגּוֹיִם: הֲשִׁיבֵנוּ יהוה אֵלֶיךָ וְנָשׁוּבָה. חַדֵּשׁ יָמֵינוּ כְּקֶדֶם:

For Elul (*Virgo*):
God is my light and my release,
Whom shall I fear?
God is the strength of my life,
Of whom shall I be afraid?
One thing I desire of God, the thing I seek,
To live in the house of God all the days of my life.
(*Psalm 27:1, 4*)

יהוה אוֹרִי וְיִשְׁעִי
מִמִּי אִירָא
יהוה מָעוֹז חַיַּי
מִמִּי אֶפְחָד:
אַחַת שָׁאַלְתִּי מֵאֵת־יהוה
אוֹתָהּ אֲבַקֵּשׁ שִׁבְתִּי בְּבֵית־יהוה כָּל־יְמֵי חַיַּי:

SHABBAT שַׁבָּת

This celebration of Jewish history, family and community takes place every week, from sunset on Friday to sunset on Saturday. As the mainstay of Jewish life, it provides an opportunity for rest and renewed commitment to our Covenant with God.

On Friday night.

For giving tzedakah (*creating a just society by performing a good deed*):

Blessed are You, Source of all Life, making us holy through Your Commandments and commanding us to do tzedakah.

בָּרוּךְ אַתָּה יהוה אֱלֹהֵינוּ מֶלֶךְ הָעוֹלָם
אֲשֶׁר קִדְּשָׁנוּ בְּמִצְוֹתָיו וְצִוָּנוּ עַל
הַצְּדָקָה:

Before lighting candles:

Peace to you, messengers of God, messengers of the Most High who rules above all, the Holy One who is blessed.
Enter in Peace, messengers of God, messengers of the Most High who rules above all, the Holy One who is blessed.
Bless me with Peace, messengers of God, messengers of the Most High who rules above all, the Holy One who is blessed.
Leave us with Peace, messengers of God, messengers of the Most High who rules above all, the Holy One who is blessed.

שָׁלוֹם עֲלֵיכֶם מַלְאֲכֵי הַשָּׁרֵת מַלְאֲכֵי
עֶלְיוֹן מִמֶּלֶךְ מַלְכֵי הַמְּלָכִים הַקָּדוֹשׁ
בָּרוּךְ הוּא:
בּוֹאֲכֶם לְשָׁלוֹם מַלְאֲכֵי הַשָּׁלוֹם
מַלְאֲכֵי עֶלְיוֹן מִמֶּלֶךְ מַלְכֵי הַמְּלָכִים
הַקָּדוֹשׁ בָּרוּךְ הוּא:
בָּרְכוּנִי לְשָׁלוֹם מַלְאֲכֵי הַשָּׁלוֹם
מַלְאֲכֵי עֶלְיוֹן מִמֶּלֶךְ מַלְכֵי הַמְּלָכִים
הַקָּדוֹשׁ בָּרוּךְ הוּא:
צֵאתְכֶם לְשָׁלוֹם מַלְאֲכֵי הַשָּׁלוֹם
מַלְאֲכֵי עֶלְיוֹן מִמֶּלֶךְ מַלְכֵי הַמְּלָכִים
הַקָּדוֹשׁ בָּרוּךְ הוּא:

After lighting candles:

Blessed are You, Source of all Life, making us holy through Your Commandments and commanding us to light these Shabbat candles.

בָּרוּךְ אַתָּה יהוה אֱלֹהֵינוּ מֶלֶךְ הָעוֹלָם
אֲשֶׁר קִדְּשָׁנוּ בְּמִצְוֹתָיו וְצִוָּנוּ לְהַדְלִיק
נֵר שֶׁל שַׁבָּת:

On blessing children:

May God make you grow like Ephraim and Manasseh.

יְשִׂמְךָ אֱלֹהִים כְּאֶפְרַיִם וְכִמְנַשֶּׁה:

May God make you grow like Sarah, Rebecca, Rachel and Leah.

יְשִׂמֵךְ אֱלֹהִים כְּשָׂרָה רִבְקָה רָחֵל וְלֵאָה:

May God bless you and help you to see all the blessings in your life.
May you feel God's presence near you at all times.
May God give you peace and help you to bring peace to your own soul, to your family and to all the world.

יְבָרֶכְךָ יְהֹוָה וְיִשְׁמְרֶךָ:
יָאֵר יְהֹוָה פָּנָיו אֵלֶיךָ וִיחֻנֶּךָּ:
יִשָּׂא יְהֹוָה פָּנָיו אֵלֶיךָ
וְיָשֵׂם לְךָ שָׁלוֹם:

On blessing a partner:

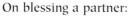

For a woman:
A woman of worth is hard to find,
For she is more precious than rubies.
Her husband trusts her in his heart,
Without losing from it.
All the days of her life,
She brings him good, not harm.
Her hands are open to the poor,
Reaching out to those in need.
She is clothed with strength and dignity,
And laughs about times to come.
Her words are words of wisdom,
Using the language of compassion.
She looks after her household,
And does not remain passive.
Her children rise to revere her
And her husband sings her praises.
Many women have done great deeds,
But you surpass them all.
Charm is a delusion and beauty fades.
The woman who reveres God is to be praised.

אֵשֶׁת חַיִל מִי יִמְצָא וְרָחֹק
מִפְּנִינִים מִכְרָהּ:
בָּטַח בָּהּ לֵב
בַּעְלָהּ וְשָׁלָל לֹא יֶחְסָר:
גְּמָלַתְהוּ טוֹב וְלֹא־רָע
כֹּל יְמֵי חַיֶּיהָ:
טָעֲמָה כִּי־טוֹב סַחְרָהּ
לֹא־יִכְבֶּה בַלַּיְלָה נֵרָהּ:
כַּפָּהּ פָּרְשָׂה לֶעָנִי וְיָדֶיהָ
שִׁלְּחָה לָאֶבְיוֹן:
עוֹז־וְהָדָר לְבוּשָׁהּ
וַתִּשְׂחַק לְיוֹם אַחֲרוֹן:
פִּיהָ פָּתְחָה בְחָכְמָה
וְתוֹרַת־חֶסֶד עַל־לְשׁוֹנָהּ:
צוֹפִיָּה הֲלִיכוֹת בֵּיתָהּ
וְלֶחֶם עַצְלוּת לֹא תֹאכֵל:
קָמוּ בָנֶיהָ וַיְאַשְּׁרוּהָ
בַּעְלָהּ וַיְהַלְלָהּ:
רַבּוֹת בָּנוֹת עָשׂוּ חָיִל
וְאַתְּ עָלִית עַל־כֻּלָּנָה:
שֶׁקֶר הַחֵן וְהֶבֶל הַיֹּפִי

Esteem her for the work of her hands,
And her own good deeds will praise her
in public.
(*Proverbs, 31*)

אֵשָׁה יִרְאַת־יְהוָה
הִיא תִתְהַלָּל:
תְּנוּ־לָהּ מִפְּרִי יָדֶיהָ וִיהַלְלוּהָ בַשְּׁעָרִים
מַעֲשֶׂיהָ:

For a man:
Happy is the man who reveres God,
Who delights in doing God's Commands.
His descendants will be respected in the land,
The generation of the virtuous will be blessed.
His house prospers and his righteousness
endures for ever.
Light shines in the darkness for the upright,
He is gracious, merciful and just.
It is good when a man is generous,
And conducts his business honestly.
For a righteous man will never stray,
He will be remembered for it always.
He is not fearful of hearing evil,
His heart is faithful and trusting in God.
His heart is steady,
He is not afraid to see his shadow.
He has given freely to the poor,
His goodness continues on.
His whole life is virtuous.
(*Psalm 112:1–9*)

אַשְׁרֵי־אִישׁ יָרֵא אֶת־יְהוָה
בְּמִצְוֹתָיו חָפֵץ מְאֹד:
גִּבּוֹר בָּאָרֶץ יִהְיֶה זַרְעוֹ
דּוֹר יְשָׁרִים יְבֹרָךְ:
הוֹן־וָעֹשֶׁר בְּבֵיתוֹ
וְצִדְקָתוֹ עֹמֶדֶת לָעַד:
זָרַח בַּחֹשֶׁךְ אוֹר לַיְשָׁרִים
חַנּוּן וְרַחוּם וְצַדִּיק:
טוֹב אִישׁ חוֹנֵן וּמַלְוֶה
יְכַלְכֵּל דְּבָרָיו בְּמִשְׁפָּט:
כִּי־לְעוֹלָם לֹא יִמּוֹט
לְזֵכֶר עוֹלָם יִהְיֶה צַדִּיק:
מִשְּׁמוּעָה רָעָה לֹא יִירָא
נָכוֹן לִבּוֹ בָּטֻחַ בַּיהוָה:
סָמוּךְ לִבּוֹ לֹא יִירָא
עַד אֲשֶׁר־יִרְאֶה בְצָרָיו:
פִּזַּר נָתַן לָאֶבְיוֹנִים
צִדְקָתוֹ עֹמֶדֶת לָעַד:
קַרְנוֹ תָּרוּם בְּכָבוֹד:

On drinking wine:
There was evening and there was morning,
the sixth day. The Heavens and the Earth
and all that is within them were completed.

וַיְהִי עֶרֶב וַיְהִי בֹקֶר יוֹם הַשִּׁשִּׁי: וַיְכֻלּוּ
הַשָּׁמַיִם וְהָאָרֶץ וְכָל צְבָאָם:

And on the seventh day, God finished all the work which God had made, and rested on the seventh day after all the work of creation. And God blessed the seventh day and set it apart, because on it God rested from all the work that God had created and established.

Blessed are You, Source of all Life, creating the fruit of the vine.

Blessed are You, Source of all Life, making us holy through Your Commandments and delighting in us.

You have given us this holy Shabbat with love as a reminder of the act of creation. For it is the most important day of all the festivals, also reminding us of the Exodus from Egypt. As You embrace us amongst all peoples, You have given us this Shabbat with love and delight.

Blessed are You, You make Shabbat holy.

On washing hands:

Blessed are You, Source of all Life, making us holy through Your Commandments, and commanding us to cleanse our hands.

On eating challah (*the braided bread used at* Shabbat):

Blessed are You, Source of all Life, bringing forth bread from the earth.

Kiddush for Shabbat morning (*the sanctification of the* Shabbat *day*):

The children of Israel shall keep Shabbat, observing Shabbat as a Covenant for all time and for all generations. It is a sign between

וַיְכַל אֱלֹהִים בַּיּוֹם הַשְּׁבִיעִי מְלַאכְתּוֹ אֲשֶׁר עָשָׂה וַיִּשְׁבֹּת בַּיּוֹם הַשְּׁבִיעִי מִכָּל מְלַאכְתּוֹ אֲשֶׁר עָשָׂה: וַיְבָרֶךְ אֱלֹהִים אֶת יוֹם הַשְּׁבִיעִי וַיְקַדֵּשׁ אֹתוֹ כִּי בוֹ שָׁבַת מִכָּל מְלַאכְתּוֹ אֲשֶׁר בָּרָא אֱלֹהִים לַעֲשׂוֹת:

בָּרוּךְ אַתָּה יהוה אֱלֹהֵינוּ מֶלֶךְ הָעוֹלָם בּוֹרֵא פְּרִי הַגָּפֶן:
בָּרוּךְ אַתָּה יהוה אֱלֹהֵינוּ מֶלֶךְ הָעוֹלָם אֲשֶׁר קִדְּשָׁנוּ בְּמִצְוֹתָיו וְרָצָה בָנוּ וְשַׁבַּת קָדְשׁוֹ בְּאַהֲבָה וּבְרָצוֹן הִנְחִילָנוּ זִכָּרוֹן לְמַעֲשֵׂה בְרֵאשִׁית
כִּי הוּא יוֹם תְּחִלָּה לְמִקְרָאֵי קֹדֶשׁ זֵכֶר לִיצִיאַת מִצְרָיִם.
כִּי בָנוּ בָחַרְתָּ וְאוֹתָנוּ קִדַּשְׁתָּ מִכָּל הָעַמִּים וְשַׁבַּת קָדְשְׁךָ בְּאַהֲבָה וּבְרָצוֹן הִנְחַלְתָּנוּ.
בָּרוּךְ אַתָּה יהוה מְקַדֵּשׁ הַשַּׁבָּת:

בָּרוּךְ אַתָּה יהוה אֱלֹהֵינוּ מֶלֶךְ הָעוֹלָם אֲשֶׁר קִדְּשָׁנוּ בְּמִצְוֹתָיו וְצִוָּנוּ עַל נְטִילַת יָדָיִם:

בָּרוּךְ אַתָּה יהוה אֱלֹהֵינוּ מֶלֶךְ הָעוֹלָם הַמּוֹצִיא לֶחֶם מִן הָאָרֶץ:

וְשָׁמְרוּ בְנֵי יִשְׂרָאֵל אֶת הַשַּׁבָּת לַעֲשׂוֹת אֶת הַשַּׁבָּת לְדֹרֹתָם בְּרִית עוֹלָם: בֵּינִי וּבֵין בְּנֵי יִשְׂרָאֵל אוֹת הִיא לְעֹלָם כִּי שֵׁשֶׁת יָמִים

God and the children of Israel, for in six days God made the heavens and the earth and on the seventh day, God rested from all the work and was refreshed.

Remember the Shabbat and keep it holy. Six days you shall toil and do all your work but the seventh shall be a Shabbat for the Eternal God. That day you shall not work: neither you, your son, your daughter, your hired help, nor your animals, nor the stranger who lives with you. For in six days, God made the heavens and the earth, the seas and all that is in them, and God rested on the seventh day. Therefore God blessed the Shabbat and made it holy.

Blessed are You, Source of all Life, creating the fruit of the vine.

Blessed are You, Source of all Life, bringing forth food out of the earth.

For Havdalah (*the ceremony of separation between* Shabbat *and the six days of the week*):
See how God is my salvation.
I shall trust and not be afraid, for God is my strength and my song and has become my salvation.
You shall draw water with joy from the wells of salvation.
Deliverance comes from God; Your blessing on Your people.
God of all creation is with us, the God of Jacob is our refuge.
Our people have had light and joy,

עָשָׂה יְהוָה אֶת הַשָּׁמַיִם וְאֶת הָאָרֶץ
וּבַיּוֹם הַשְּׁבִיעִי שָׁבַת וַיִּנָּפַשׁ

זָכוֹר אֶת־יוֹם הַשַּׁבָּת לְקַדְּשׁוֹ: שֵׁשֶׁת
יָמִים תַּעֲבֹד וְעָשִׂיתָ כָּל־מְלַאכְתֶּךָ:
וְיוֹם הַשְּׁבִיעִי שַׁבָּת לַיהוָה אֱלֹהֶיךָ
לֹא־תַעֲשֶׂה כָל־מְלָאכָה אַתָּה וּבִנְךָ
וּבִתֶּךָ עַבְדְּךָ וַאֲמָתְךָ וּבְהֶמְתֶּךָ וְגֵרְךָ
אֲשֶׁר בִּשְׁעָרֶיךָ: כִּי שֵׁשֶׁת־יָמִים עָשָׂה
יְהוָה אֶת־הַשָּׁמַיִם וְאֶת־הָאָרֶץ אֶת־הַיָּם
וְאֶת־כָּל־אֲשֶׁר־בָּם וַיָּנַח בַּיּוֹם
הַשְּׁבִיעִי עַל־כֵּן בֵּרַךְ יְהוָה אֶת־יוֹם
הַשַּׁבָּת וַיְקַדְּשֵׁהוּ:

בָּרוּךְ אַתָּה יְהוָה אֱלֹהֵינוּ מֶלֶךְ הָעוֹלָם
בּוֹרֵא פְּרִי הַגָּפֶן:

בָּרוּךְ אַתָּה יְהוָה אֱלֹהֵינוּ מֶלֶךְ הָעוֹלָם
הַמּוֹצִיא לֶחֶם מִן הָאָרֶץ:

הִנֵּה אֵל יְשׁוּעָתִי אֶבְטַח
וְלֹא אֶפְחָד כִּי עָזִּי וְזִמְרָת יָהּ יְהוָה
וַיְהִי־לִי לִישׁוּעָה:
וּשְׁאַבְתֶּם מַיִם בְּשָׂשׂוֹן מִמַּעַיְנֵי הַיְשׁוּעָה:
לַיהוָה הַיְשׁוּעָה עַל עַמְּךָ בִרְכָתֶךָ
סֶלָה:
יְהוָה צְבָאוֹת עִמָּנוּ מִשְׂגָּב לָנוּ אֱלֹהֵי
יַעֲקֹב סֶלָה:
לַיְּהוּדִים הָיְתָה אוֹרָה וְשִׂמְחָה וְשָׂשׂוֹן
וִיקָר: כֵּן תִּהְיֶה לָּנוּ:
כּוֹס יְשׁוּעוֹת אֶשָּׂא וּבְשֵׁם יְהוָה אֶקְרָא:

gladness and reverence, so may it be with us.

I lift the cup of salvation and call in God's name.

Blessed are You, Source of all Life, creating the fruit of the vine.

Blessed are You, Source of all Life, creating a variety of spices.

Blessed are You, Source of all Life, creating the flames of fire.

Blessed are You, Source of all Life, separating holiness from the profane, light from darkness, Israel from the other nations, the seventh day from the six working days of the week.

Blessed are You, God, distinguishing between holiness and the profane.

בָּרוּךְ אַתָּה יהוה אֱלֹהֵינוּ מֶלֶךְ הָעוֹלָם
בּוֹרֵא פְּרִי הַגָּפֶן:
בָּרוּךְ אַתָּה יהוה אֱלֹהֵינוּ מֶלֶךְ הָעוֹלָם
בּוֹרֵא מִינֵי בְשָׂמִים:
בָּרוּךְ אַתָּה יהוה אֱלֹהֵינוּ מֶלֶךְ הָעוֹלָם
בּוֹרֵא מְאוֹרֵי הָאֵשׁ:
בָּרוּךְ אַתָּה יהוה אֱלֹהֵינוּ מֶלֶךְ הָעוֹלָם
הַמַּבְדִּיל בֵּין קֹדֶשׁ לְחוֹל בֵּין
אוֹר לְחֹשֶׁךְ בֵּין יִשְׂרָאֵל לָעַמִּים. בֵּין
יוֹם הַשְּׁבִיעִי לְשֵׁשֶׁת יְמֵי הַמַּעֲשֶׂה.
בָּרוּךְ אַתָּה יהוה הַמַּבְדִּיל בֵּין קֹדֶשׁ
לְחוֹל:

Elijah the prophet.

Elijah the Tishbite.

Elijah the man of Gilead.

May he come soon, to fulfil the promise of David and bring the Messiah.

A Happy Week!

אֵלִיָּהוּ הַנָּבִיא
אֵלִיָּהוּ הַתִּשְׁבִּי
אֵלִיָּהוּ הַגִּלְעָדִי
בִּמְהֵרָה יָבֹא אֵלֵינוּ עִם מָשִׁיחַ בֶּן־
דָּוִד:

שָׁבוּעַ טוֹב

This is the Jewish New Year ceremony that marks the beginning of ten days of reflection on the past year, as well as atonement for personal sins. The shofar, or ram's horn, is sounded repeatedly in the synagogue during Rosh Hashanah.

For the eve of Rosh Hashanah:

Remember us for life, for You delight in life.
Inscribe us in the book of life, for Your sake, O God of life.

זָכְרֵנוּ לַחַיִּים מֶלֶךְ חָפֵץ בַּחַיִּים
וְכָתְבֵנוּ בְּסֵפֶר הַחַיִּים
לְמַעַנְךָ אֱלֹהִים חַיִּים:

Blessed are You, Source of all Life, making us holy through Your Commandments and commanding us to light the festival lights.

בָּרוּךְ אַתָּה יהוה אֱלֹהֵינוּ מֶלֶךְ הָעוֹלָם
אֲשֶׁר קִדְּשָׁנוּ בְּמִצְוֹתָיו וְצִוָּנוּ לְהַדְלִיק נֵר
שֶׁל (שַׁבָּת וְשֶׁל) יוֹם טוֹב:

For dipping an apple into honey:

Blessed are You, Source of all Life, creating fruit from the tree.

בָּרוּךְ אַתָּה יהוה אֱלֹהֵינוּ מֶלֶךְ הָעוֹלָם
בּוֹרֵא פְּרִי הָעֵץ:

May it be Your will, our God and God of our ancestors, that the new year will be for us a good and sweet one.

יְהִי רָצוֹן מִלְּפָנֶיךָ יהוה אֱלֹהֵינוּ וֵאלֹהֵי
אֲבוֹתֵינוּ שֶׁתְּחַדֵּשׁ עָלֵינוּ שָׁנָה טוֹבָה
וּמְתוּקָה:

May you be recorded in the book of life for a good and happy year.

לְשָׁנָה טוֹבָה תִּכָּתֵבוּ

Kiddush for festival evenings:

Blessed are You, Source of all Life, creating the fruit of the vine.
Blessed are You, Source of all Life, choosing us from among all peoples and nurturing us in order to make us holy through doing Your Commands.
You, our God, have given us seasons of joy and festivals of gladness on this holy day of Rosh Hashanah as a remembrance of the Exodus from Egypt. You choose to make us holy among all peoples by giving us the

בָּרוּךְ אַתָּה יהוה אֱלֹהֵינוּ מֶלֶךְ הָעוֹלָם
בּוֹרֵא פְּרִי הַגָּפֶן:
בָּרוּךְ אַתָּה יהוה אֱלֹהֵינוּ מֶלֶךְ הָעוֹלָם
אֲשֶׁר בָּחַר בָּנוּ מִכָּל עָם וְרוֹמְמָנוּ מִכָּל
לָשׁוֹן וְקִדְּשָׁנוּ בְּמִצְוֹתָיו.
וַתִּתֶּן לָנוּ יהוה אֱלֹהֵינוּ בְּאַהֲבָה (שַׁבָּתוֹת
לִמְנוּחָה) מוֹעֲדִים לְשִׂמְחָה חַגִּים וּזְמַנִּים
לְשָׂשׂוֹן אֶת יוֹם (הַשַּׁבָּת הַזֶּה וְאֶת יוֹם
הַזֶּה (בְּאַהֲבָה) מִקְרָא קֹדֶשׁ זֵכֶר לִיצִיאַת
מִצְרָיִם. כִּי בָנוּ בָחַרְתָּ וְאוֹתָנוּ קִדַּשְׁתָּ
מִכָּל הָעַמִּים (וְשַׁבָּת) וּמוֹעֲדֵי קָדְשְׁךָ

inheritance of our festivals for joy and
gladness.
Blessed are You, God, making holy Israel
and the festivals.

Tashlich on Rosh Hashanah (the release
of past sins through the symbolic act of
throwing bread into water):

Who is like You, God, forgiving iniquity and
pardoning the sins of Your people? You do not
remain angry but You delight in loving
kindness. You will have compassion upon us
again, subduing our sins. You will cast all our
sins into the depths of the sea. You will show
faithfulness to Jacob and enduring love to
Abraham, as You promised our ancestors from
days of old.
(Micah, 7:18–20)

None shall hurt or destroy in all my holy
mountain, for the love of God shall fill the
earth as the waters cover the sea.
(Isaiah, 11:9)

How can I escape Your spirit?
How can I flee Your presence?
If I ascend to the heavens, You are there,
If I descend to the depths, You are there,
If I mount the wings of the dawn
Or dwell beyond the sea,
Even there You shall lead me
And Your right hand shall hold me fast.
(Psalm 139:7–10)

(בְּאַהֲבָה וּבְרָצוֹן) בְּשִׂמְחָה וּבְשָׂשׂוֹן
הִנְחַלְתָּנוּ. בָּרוּךְ אַתָּה יהוה מְקַדֵּשׁ
(הַשַּׁבָּת וְ) יִשְׂרָאֵל וְהַזְּמַנִּים:

מִי־אֵל כָּמוֹךָ נֹשֵׂא עָוֹן וְעֹבֵר עַל־פֶּשַׁע
לִשְׁאֵרִית נַחֲלָתוֹ לֹא־הֶחֱזִיק לָעַד אַפּוֹ
כִּי־חָפֵץ חֶסֶד הוּא: יָשׁוּב יְרַחֲמֵנוּ יִכְבֹּשׁ
עֲוֹנֹתֵינוּ וְתַשְׁלִיךְ בִּמְצֻלוֹת יָם כָּל־
חַטֹּאתָם: תִּתֵּן אֱמֶת לְיַעֲקֹב חֶסֶד
לְאַבְרָהָם אֲשֶׁר־נִשְׁבַּעְתָּ לַאֲבֹתֵינוּ מִימֵי
קֶדֶם:

לֹא־יָרֵעוּ וְלֹא־יַשְׁחִיתוּ בְּכָל־הַר קָדְשִׁי
כִּי־מָלְאָה הָאָרֶץ דֵּעָה אֶת־יהוה כַּמַּיִם
לַיָּם מְכַסִּים:

אָנָה אֵלֵךְ מֵרוּחֶךָ
וְאָנָה מִפָּנֶיךָ אֶבְרָח:
אִם־אֶסַּק שָׁמַיִם שָׁם אָתָּה
וְאַצִּיעָה שְּׁאוֹל הִנֶּךָ:
אֶשָּׂא כַנְפֵי־שָׁחַר אֶשְׁכְּנָה
בְּאַחֲרִית יָם: גַּם־שָׁם יָדְךָ
תַנְחֵנִי וְתֹאחֲזֵנִי יְמִינֶךָ:

YOM KIPPUR

יוֹם כִּפּוּר

The holiest day of the Jewish calendar, Yom Kippur *includes ceremonies that require sacrifice and atonement in order to seek forgiveness for wrongdoing and personal faults.*

For Kol Nidrei (*the evening of* Yom Kippur):

Blessed are You, Source of all Life and Repentance, making us holy through Your Commandments and commanding us to light the Yom Kippur lights.

בָּרוּךְ אַתָּה יהוה אֱלֹהֵינוּ מֶלֶךְ הָעוֹלָם
אֲשֶׁר קִדְּשָׁנוּ בְּמִצְוֹתָיו וְצִוָּנוּ לְהַדְלִיק נֵר
שֶׁל (שַׁבָּת וְשֶׁל) יוֹם הַכִּפּוּרִים:

Those who are required to eat on Yom Kippur say:

Blessed are You, Source of all Life and Repentance, making us holy through Your Commandments and commanding us to preserve life.

May you be sealed in the book of life.

בָּרוּךְ אַתָּה יהוה אֱלֹהֵינוּ מֶלֶךְ הָעוֹלָם
אֲשֶׁר קִדְּשָׁנוּ בְּמִצְוֹתָיו וְצִוָּנוּ עַל פִּקוּחַ
נֶפֶשׁ:

לְשָׁנָה טוֹבָה תֵּחָתֵמוּ

Breaking the fast:

Blessed are You, Source of all Life, bringing bread from out of the earth.

בָּרוּךְ אַתָּה יהוה אֱלֹהֵינוּ מֶלֶךְ הָעוֹלָם
הַמּוֹצִיא לֶחֶם מִן הָאָרֶץ:

For meditation at Yom Kippur:

O God, pardon the sins, iniquities and transgressions which I have committed before You, I and my household. As it has been said: On this day atonement shall be made for you, to purify you; you shall be cleansed from all your sins before the Eternal.

(*Mishnah Yoma, 3:8*)

אָנָּא הַשֵּׁם חָטָאתִי עָוִיתִי פָּשַׁעְתִּי לְפָנֶיךָ
אֲנִי וּבֵיתִי אָנָּא בַּשֵּׁם כַּפֶּר נָא לַחֲטָאִים
וְלַעֲוֹנוֹת וְלַפְּשָׁעִים שֶׁחָטָאתִי וְשֶׁעָוִיתִי
וְשֶׁפָּשַׁעְתִּי לְפָנֶיךָ אֲנִי וּבֵיתִי כַּכָּתוּב
בְּתוֹרַת מֹשֶׁה עַבְדְּךָ מִפִּי כְבוֹדֶךָ כִּי בַיּוֹם
הַזֶּה יְכַפֵּר עֲלֵיכֶם לְטַהֵר אֶתְכֶם מִכֹּל
חַטֹּאתֵיכֶם לִפְנֵי יהוה:

SUKKOT

This festival gives thanks for nature's bounty and God's historic protection. During the week of Sukkot, some of us build and live in a sukkah, a temporary shelter open to the sky. Akin to the dwelling the people of Israel built in the wilderness while journeying to the Promised Land, it reminds us of the fragility and transient nature of all living things. On entering a sukkah, we wave a lulav, a bouquet of palm, myrtle, willow and etrog (citron).

Beginning to build a sukkah:

Blessed are You, Source of all Life, making us holy through Your Commandments and commanding us to build a sukkah.

בָּרוּךְ אַתָּה יהוה אֱלֹהֵינוּ מֶלֶךְ הָעוֹלָם אֲשֶׁר קִדְּשָׁנוּ בְּמִצְוֹתָיו וְצִוָּנוּ לִבְנוֹת סֻכָּה:

Entering a sukkah :

Blessed are You, Source of all Life, making us holy through Your Commandments and commanding us to wave the lulav.

בָּרוּךְ אַתָּה יהוה אֱלֹהֵינוּ מֶלֶךְ הָעוֹלָם אֲשֶׁר קִדְּשָׁנוּ בְּמִצְוֹתָיו וְצִוָּנוּ עַל נְטִילַת לוּלָב:

Blessed are You, Source of all Life, making us holy through Your Commandments and commanding us to assemble in the sukkah.

בָּרוּךְ אַתָּה יְיָ אֱלֹהֵינוּ מֶלֶךְ הָעוֹלָם אֲשֶׁר קִדְּשָׁנוּ בְּמִצְוֹתָיו וְצִוָּנוּ לֵישֵׁב בַּסֻּכָּה:

This eight-day festival commemorates the ancient struggle to uphold a sovereign Jewish state and its religious freedom. The festival is celebrated by the lighting of the eight-branched ritual lamp known as a menorah.

For the eight nights of Chanukah:

Blessed are You, Source of all Life, making us holy through Your Commandments and commanding us to kindle the lights of Chanukah.

בָּרוּךְ אַתָּה יהוה אֱלֹהֵינוּ מֶלֶךְ הָעוֹלָם אֲשֶׁר קִדְּשָׁנוּ בְּמִצְוֹתָיו וְצִוָּנוּ לְהַדְלִיק נֵר שֶׁל חֲנֻכָּה:

Blessed are You, Source of all Life, making miracles for our ancestors during this season long ago.

בָּרוּךְ אַתָּה יהוה אֱלֹהֵינוּ מֶלֶךְ הָעוֹלָם שֶׁעָשָׂה נִסִּים לַאֲבוֹתֵינוּ בַּיָּמִים הָהֵם בַּזְּמַן הַזֶּה:

Blessed are You, Source of all Life, giving us life, sustaining us and enabling us to reach this special time.

בָּרוּךְ אַתָּה יהוה אֱלֹהֵינוּ מֶלֶךְ הָעוֹלָם שֶׁהֶחֱיָנוּ וְקִיְּמָנוּ וְהִגִּיעָנוּ לַזְּמַן הַזֶּה:

We kindle these lights for the miracles, wonders and victories that You performed for our ancestors during this season long ago through Your ordained priests. These lights are special during the eight days of Chanukah: we are instructed to use them only for looking at, in order to thank You for the miracles, wonders and victories.

הַנֵּרוֹת הַלָּלוּ אֲנַחְנוּ מַדְלִיקִים עַל הַנִּסִּים וְעַל הַנִּפְלָאוֹת וְעַל הַתְּשׁוּעוֹת וְעַל הַמִּלְחָמוֹת שֶׁעָשִׂיתָ לַאֲבוֹתֵינוּ בַּיָּמִים הָהֵם בַּזְּמַן הַזֶּה עַל יְדֵי כֹּהֲנֶיךָ הַקְּדוֹשִׁים וְכָל שְׁמוֹנַת יְמֵי חֲנֻכָּה הַנֵּרוֹת הַלָּלוּ קֹדֶשׁ הֵם וְאֵין לָנוּ רְשׁוּת לְהִשְׁתַּמֵּשׁ בָּהֶם אֶלָּא לִרְאוֹתָם בִּלְבָד כְּדֵי לְהוֹדוֹת וּלְהַלֵּל לְשִׁמְךָ הַגָּדוֹל עַל נִסֶּיךָ וְעַל נִפְלְאוֹתֶיךָ וְעַל יְשׁוּעָתֶךָ:

Rock of my salvation, to You praise is due. Establish Your house of prayer and let thanksgiving be offered there. The time will come when You will end all hurt and enemies will cease to be. Then I will sing and celebrate the dedication of Your sanctuary.

מָעוֹז צוּר יְשׁוּעָתִי לְךָ נָאֶה לְשַׁבֵּחַ. תִּכּוֹן בֵּית תְּפִלָּתִי וְשָׁם תּוֹדָה נְזַבֵּחַ. לְעֵת תָּכִין מַטְבֵּחַ מִצָּר הַמְנַבֵּחַ. אָז אֶגְמֹר בְּשִׁיר מִזְמוֹר חֲנֻכַּת הַמִּזְבֵּחַ:

This festival celebrates the role of Queen Esther in saving the Jewish people from persecution. Purim is traditionally a happy time with fun activities for children and adults. It is also a time for charitable acts.

Mishloach Manot for Purim (*the traditional custom of distributing gifts of food on Purim*):
The Jews of the villages make the fourteenth day of the month of Adar a day of gladness and feasting and holiday, and of sending gifts one to another.
(*Esther, 9:19*)

עַל־כֵּן הַיְּהוּדִים הַפְּרוֹזִים הַיֹּשְׁבִים בְּעָרֵי
הַפְּרָזוֹת עֹשִׂים אֵת יוֹם אַרְבָּעָה עָשָׂר
לְחֹדֶשׁ אֲדָר שִׂמְחָה וּמִשְׁתֶּה וְיוֹם טוֹב
וּמִשְׁלוֹחַ מָנוֹת אִישׁ לְרֵעֵהוּ׃

PESACH

פֶּסַח

This Jewish festival of freedom reminds us of the Exodus from Egypt and the subsequent rituals of the ancient Temple in Jerusalem. Today, Pesach is predominantly celebrated in the home at a ceremonial meal, called the Seder, with readings from the ancient book, the Pesach Haggadah.

Search for Hametz (*leavened products to be avoided during the Pesach week*):

Before the search:

Blessed are You, Source of all Life, making us holy through Your Commandments and commanding us to search for Hametz.

בָּרוּךְ אַתָּה יהוה אֱלֹהֵינוּ מֶלֶךְ הָעוֹלָם אֲשֶׁר קִדְּשָׁנוּ בְּמִצְוֹתָיו וְצִוָּנוּ עַל בְּעוּר חָמֵץ:

After the search:

All Hametz in my possession which I have not seen or removed or of which I am unaware, is hereby nullified and as ownerless as the dust of the earth.

כָּל חֲמִירָא וַחֲמִיעָה דְּאִכָּא בִרְשׁוּתִי דְּלָא חֲמִתֵּהּ וּדְלָא בְעַרְתֵּהּ וּדְלָא יְדַעְנָא לֵהּ לִבָּטֵל וְלֶהֱוֵי הֶפְקֵר כְּעַפְרָא דְאַרְעָא

Counting of the Omer (*the period of time between Pesach and Shavuot, counted daily in synagogues*):

You shall count seven weeks from the day after Pesach when an omer of grain is to be brought as an offering, so that the day after the seventh week will make it fifty days.

וּסְפַרְתֶּם לָכֶם מִמָּחֳרַת הַשַּׁבָּת מִיּוֹם הֲבִיאֲכֶם אֶת עֹמֶר הַתְּנוּפָה שֶׁבַע שַׁבָּתוֹת תְּמִימֹת תִּהְיֶינָה עַד מִמָּחֳרַת הַשַּׁבָּת הַשְּׁבִיעִת תִּסְפְּרוּ חֲמִשִּׁים יוֹם:

Blessed are You, Source of all Life, making us holy through Your Commandments and commanding us to count the days of the Omer. This is the .... day being .... weeks and .... days of the Omer.

בָּרוּךְ אַתָּה יהוה אֱלֹהֵינוּ מֶלֶךְ הָעוֹלָם אֲשֶׁר קִדְּשָׁנוּ בְּמִצְוֹתָיו וְצִוָּנוּ עַל סְפִירַת הָעֹמֶר: הַיּוֹם . . . יוֹם שֶׁהֵם . . . שָׁבוּעוֹת . . . יָמִים לָעֹמֶר:

This festival celebrates the gift of Torah as a source of wisdom, lore and law. Study of the Torah is a special feature of Shavuot, marked by a Tikkun Leyl Shavuot (a traditional midnight study session on the eve of Shavuot) and the graduation of students of Torah.

For Tikkun Leyl Shavuot:

Blessed are You, Source of all Life, choosing us from all peoples and giving us Your Torah. Blessed are You, God, giving us Torah.

בָּרוּךְ אַתָּה יהוה אֱלֹהֵינוּ מֶלֶךְ הָעוֹלָם אֲשֶׁר בָּחַר בָּנוּ מִכָּל הָעַמִּים וְנָתַן לָנוּ אֶת תּוֹרָתוֹ. בָּרוּךְ אַתָּה יהוה נוֹתֵן הַתּוֹרָה:

Blessed are You, Source of all Life, giving us true teachings and planting within us everlasting life. Blessed are You, God, giving us Torah.

בָּרוּךְ אַתָּה יהוה אֱלֹהֵינוּ מֶלֶךְ הָעוֹלָם אֲשֶׁר נָתַן לָנוּ תּוֹרַת אֱמֶת וְחַיֵּי עוֹלָם נָטַע בְּתוֹכֵנוּ. בָּרוּךְ אַתָּה יהוה נוֹתֵן הַתּוֹרָה:

PRAYERS AND BLESSINGS FOR EVERY DAY

If you enjoy something in this world without first saying a blessing,
it is as if you stole it - TALMUD BERACHOT, 35A

In Judaism, it is traditional to say blessings of thanksgiving every day. Some are recited prior to eating or drinking (*birkat hanehenin*); some are recited before rituals (*birkat hamitzvot*); and others express praise and thanks to God (*birkat hodaah*). Reciting these blessings, we show our appreciation for the beauty of the world. Every joyful occasion, striking phenomenon of nature, or performance of a *mitzvah* offers the opportunity to be spiritually aware. In this way, we sanctify our daily activities, bringing God into our lives.

There are also prayers and blessings for meditation and healing which recognize that we exist in partnership with God. As we meditate on what afflicts us, we can draw comfort in knowing that we are not alone. By seeking God's support, we become empowered with strength and hope. Whether we pray privately or with others, prayers for healing enable us to understand ourselves better, and teach us about compassion and support for others.

Though many of these prayers and blessings can be recited as part of a fixed daily routine, their ceremonial nature should not overshadow their meaning. Rather we should recite them with *kavanah*, intention behind the recitation, which allows depth of meaning. The eleventh-century philosopher, Bachya Ibn Pakuda, wrote: 'For you must know that words are a matter of the tongue, but meaning is a matter of the heart. The words are the body of the prayer, but the meaning is its soul.' As the Hassidic masters used to say, we pray that we might pray well.

THANKSGIVING

For Birkat Hamazon (*a series of traditional blessings said after meals in praise of God's abundant world and the land of Israel*):

A Song of Pilgrimage.

When God restored the exiles of Zion, we felt as in a dream.

Our mouths were filled with laughter, our tongues with joyful song.

Then it was said among the nations: Their God has done great things for them.

God had done great things for us, and we rejoiced.

Once more, Eternal One, restore our exiles, as streams revive the desert.

Then those who sow in tears shall reap in joy.

Then those who go forth weeping, as they bear their bags of seed, shall sing for joy as they return, bringing home their sheaves.

שִׁיר הַמַּעֲלוֹת בְּשׁוּב
יהוה אֶת שִׁיבַת צִיּוֹן
הָיִינוּ כְּחֹלְמִים:
אָז יִמָּלֵא שְׂחוֹק פִּינוּ וּלְשׁוֹנֵנוּ רִנָּה
אָז יֹאמְרוּ בַגּוֹיִם
הִגְדִּיל יהוה לַעֲשׂוֹת עִם־אֵלֶּה:
הִגְדִּיל יהוה לַעֲשׂוֹת עִמָּנוּ
הָיִינוּ שְׂמֵחִים: שׁוּבָה יהוה
אֶת־שְׁבִיתֵנוּ כַּאֲפִיקִים בַּנֶּגֶב:
הַזֹּרְעִים בְּדִמְעָה בְּרִנָּה יִקְצֹרוּ
הָלוֹךְ יֵלֵךְ וּבָכֹה נֹשֵׂא מֶשֶׁךְ־הַזָּרַע
בֹּא־יָבֹא בְרִנָּה נֹשֵׂא
אֲלֻמֹּתָיו:

Leader:

Let us praise God.

רַבּוֹתַי נְבָרֵךְ:

All:

Let God's name be praised, now and for ever.

יְהִי שֵׁם יהוה מְבֹרָךְ מֵעַתָּה וְעַד
עוֹלָם:

Leader:

Let us bless our God, of whose gifts we have eaten.

בִּרְשׁוּת רַבּוֹתַי נְבָרֵךְ שֶׁאָכַלְנוּ מִשֶּׁלּוֹ:

All:

Blessed be our God, of whose gifts we have eaten and by whose goodness we live.

בָּרוּךְ אֱלֹהֵינוּ שֶׁאָכַלְנוּ מִשֶּׁלּוֹ וּבְטוּבוֹ
חָיִינוּ:

Blessed be God, and blessed be God's name.

Blessed are You, our Eternal God, Ruler of the world, by whose goodness the whole world is sustained. With grace, love and mercy You give food for all flesh, for Your love is unending. Through Your great goodness, we have never lacked our daily bread; may we never do so, for Your great name's sake. For You feed and nourish all, You are good to all, and provide enough for all Your creatures. Blessed are You, Eternal One, Sustainer of all.

We thank You, our Eternal God, for the pleasant, good and spacious land You gave our ancestors; for leading us out of Egypt, and redeeming us from the house of bondage; for the Covenant You have sealed into our hearts; for the Torah You have taught us, and the laws You have made known to us; for Your gracious gifts of life and love; and for the food with which You sustain us each and every day. For all these things, our Eternal God, we thank and bless You. May Your name be blessed continually by every living creature, as it is written: When you have eaten and are satisfied, then bless your Eternal God for the good land that has been given you.

בָּרוּךְ הוּא וּבָרוּךְ שְׁמוֹ

בָּרוּךְ אַתָּה יהוה אֱלֹהֵינוּ מֶלֶךְ הָעוֹלָם. הַזָּן אֶת־הָעוֹלָם כֻּלּוֹ. בְּטוּבוֹ בְּחֵן בְּחֶסֶד וּבְרַחֲמִים. הוּא נוֹתֵן לֶחֶם לְכָל־ בָּשָׂר. כִּי לְעוֹלָם חַסְדּוֹ: וּבְטוּבוֹ הַגָּדוֹל תָּמִיד לֹא־חָסַר לָנוּ וְאַל־יֶחְסַר לָנוּ מָזוֹן לְעוֹלָם וָעֶד בַּעֲבוּר שְׁמוֹ הַגָּדוֹל כִּי הוּא זָן וּמְפַרְנֵס לַכֹּל וּמֵטִיב לַכֹּל וּמֵכִין מָזוֹן לְכָל־בְּרִיּוֹתָיו אֲשֶׁר בָּרָא. בָּרוּךְ אַתָּה יהוה. הַזָּן אֶת הַכֹּל:

נוֹדֶה לְךָ יהוה אֱלֹהֵינוּ עַל שֶׁהִנְחַלְתָּ לַאֲבוֹתֵינוּ אֶרֶץ חֶמְדָּה טוֹבָה וּרְחָבָה. וְעַל שֶׁהוֹצֵאתָנוּ מֵאֶרֶץ מִצְרַיִם וּפְדִיתָנוּ מִבֵּית עֲבָדִים וְעַל בְּרִיתְךָ שֶׁחָתַמְתָּ בִּלְבָבֵנוּ וְעַל תּוֹרָתְךָ שֶׁלִּמַּדְתָּנוּ. וְעַל חֻקֶּיךָ שֶׁהוֹדַעְתָּנוּ. וְעַל חַיִּים חֵן וָחֶסֶד שֶׁחוֹנַנְתָּנוּ. וְעַל אֲכִילַת מָזוֹן שָׁאַתָּה זָן וּמְפַרְנֵס אוֹתָנוּ תָּמִיד בְּכָל־יוֹם וּבְכָל־עֵת וּבְכָל־שָׁעָה: וְעַל הַכֹּל יהוה אֱלֹהֵינוּ אֲנַחְנוּ מוֹדִים לָךְ וּמְבָרְכִים אוֹתָךְ. יִתְבָּרַךְ שִׁמְךָ בְּפִי כָל־ חַי תָּמִיד לְעוֹלָם וָעֶד: כַּכָּתוּב. וְאָכַלְתָּ וְשָׂבָעְתָּ וּבֵרַכְתָּ אֶת־יהוה אֱלֹהֶיךָ עַל־ הָאָרֶץ הַטֹּבָה אֲשֶׁר נָתַן לָךְ:

Blessed are You, O God, for the land and for the food.

בָּרוּךְ אַתָּה יהוה עַל־הָאָרֶץ וְעַל הַמָּזוֹן

Blessed are You, our Eternal God, Ruler of the world, our caring God and Sovereign, mighty Creator and Redeemer, the Holy One of Jacob and the Shepherd of Israel, good and beneficent to all. Show us Your love and kindness in the future as in the past. Grant us grace and compassion, freedom and deliverance, prosperity and blessing, redemption and consolation, sustenance, life and peace; may we never lack all that we need for our good.

בָּרוּךְ אַתָּה יהוה אֱלֹהֵינוּ מֶלֶךְ הָעוֹלָם. הָאֵל אָבִינוּ מַלְכֵּנוּ אַדִירֵנוּ בּוֹרְאֵנוּ גּוֹאֲלֵנוּ יוֹצְרֵנוּ קְדוֹשֵׁנוּ קְדוֹשׁ יַעֲקֹב. רוֹעֵנוּ רוֹעֵה יִשְׂרָאֵל. הַמֶּלֶךְ הַטּוֹב וְהַמֵּטִיב לַכֹּל שֶׁבְּכָל־יוֹם וָיוֹם הוּא הֵטִיב הוּא מֵטִיב הוּא יֵיטִיב לָנוּ הוּא גְמָלָנוּ הוּא גוֹמְלֵנוּ הוּא יִגְמְלֵנוּ לָעַד. לְחֵן לְחֶסֶד וּלְרַחֲמִים וּלְרֶוַח הַצָּלָה וְהַצְלָחָה בְּרָכָה וִישׁוּעָה נֶחָמָה פַרְנָסָה וְכַלְכָּלָה

May the Merciful One bless us and all our dear ones. As our ancestors Abraham, Isaac and Jacob, Sarah, Rebecca, Rachel and Leah were blessed in all things, so may we be blessed, one and all, and let us say: Amen.

הָרַחֲמָן הוּא יְבָרֵךְ אוֹתָנוּ וְאֶת־כָּל־אֲשֶׁר לָנוּ כְּמוֹ שֶׁנִּתְבָּרְכוּ אֲבוֹתֵינוּ אַבְרָהָם יִצְחָק וְיַעֲקֹב וְאִמּוֹתֵינוּ שָׂרָה רִבְקָה רָחֵל וְלֵאָה בַּכֹּל מִכֹּל כֹּל כֵּן יְבָרֵךְ אוֹתָנוּ כֻּלָּנוּ יַחַד בִּבְרָכָה שְׁלֵמָה וְנֹאמַר אָמֵן

May God who causes peace to reign in the heavens above grant peace to us, to all Israel, and to all the world.

עֹשֶׂה שָׁלוֹם בִּמְרוֹמָיו הוּא יַעֲשֶׂה שָׁלוֹם עָלֵינוּ וְעַל כָּל יִשְׂרָאֵל וְאִמְרוּ אָמֵן

May God give strength to this people; may God bless this people with peace.

יהוה עֹז לְעַמּוֹ יִתֵּן יהוה יְבָרֵךְ אֶת עַמּוֹ בַשָּׁלוֹם

For eating vegetables:
Blessed are You, Source of all Life, creating the fruit of the earth.

בָּרוּךְ אַתָּה יהוה אֱלֹהֵינוּ מֶלֶךְ הָעוֹלָם בּוֹרֵא פְּרִי הָאֲדָמָה:

For eating other foods and drinks:
Blessed are You, Source of all Life, by whose word everything comes into being.

בָּרוּךְ אַתָּה יהוה אֱלֹהֵינוּ מֶלֶךְ הָעוֹלָם שֶׁהַכֹּל נִהְיֶה בִּדְבָרוֹ:

For smelling flowers:
Blessed are You, Source of all Life, creating scented flowers.

בָּרוּךְ אַתָּה יהוה אֱלֹהֵינוּ מֶלֶךְ הָעוֹלָם בּוֹרֵא עִשְׂבֵי בְשָׂמִים

For sweet smelling perfume:
Blessed are You, Source of all Life, creating sweet smelling oils.

בָּרוּךְ אַתָּה יהוה אֱלֹהֵינוּ מֶלֶךְ הָעוֹלָם
בּוֹרֵא שֶׁמֶן עָרֵב:

For the wonders of nature:
Blessed are You, Source of all Life, renewing the work of creation every day.

בָּרוּךְ אַתָּה יהוה אֱלֹהֵינוּ מֶלֶךְ הָעוֹלָם
עוֹשֶׂה מַעֲשֶׂה בְרֵאשִׁית

For a beautiful sight:
Blessed are You, Source of all Life, filling the world with beauty.

בָּרוּךְ אַתָּה יהוה אֱלֹהֵינוּ מֶלֶךְ הָעוֹלָם
שֶׁכָּכָה לוֹ בְּעוֹלָמוֹ

For rain:
The days of summer are gone. The rainy season is here. Its showers will gather and then pour themselves, more and more, upon the earth. Grain, wine and oil will flourish quickly. The clouds will send down rain and urge the earth to bring forth grass. Seeds and buds will grow in beauty.

יְמֵי הַקַּיִץ עָבְרוּ הַסְּתָיו בָּא מַטְרוֹתָיו
יִחֲשַׂרוּ וְעַל הָאָרֶץ יָרִיקוּ וְיִגְבְּרוּ דָּגָן
תִּירוֹשׁ וְיִצְהָר מְהֵרָה יִפְרוּ הֶעָבִים גֶּשֶׁם
יַמְטִירוּ חֶלֶד עֲשָׂבִים לָצֵאת יְמַהֲרוּ.
זֵרְעוֹנֶיהָ וְנִצֶּיהָ יַשְׁפִּרוּ.

For eating cakes or biscuits:
Blessed are You, Source of all Life, creating diverse kinds of food.

בָּרוּךְ אַתָּה יהוה אֱלֹהֵינוּ מֶלֶךְ הָעוֹלָם
בּוֹרֵא מִינֵי מְזוֹנוֹת

For eating fruits that grow on trees:
Blessed are You, Source of all Life, creating the fruit of the tree.

בָּרוּךְ אַתָּה יהוה אֱלֹהֵינוּ מֶלֶךְ הָעוֹלָם.
בּוֹרֵא פְּרִי הָעֵץ:

For hearing thunder:
Blessed are You, Source of all Life, filling the world with power and might.

בָּרוּךְ אַתָּה יהוה אֱלֹהֵינוּ מֶלֶךְ הָעוֹלָם.
שֶׁכֹּחוֹ וּגְבוּרָתוֹ מָלֵא עוֹלָם:

For seeing a rainbow:
Blessed are You, Source of all Life, remembering Your Covenant and preserving Your promise to Noah.

בָּרוּךְ אַתָּה יהוה אֱלֹהֵינוּ מֶלֶךְ הָעוֹלָם.
זוֹכֵר בְּרִיתוֹ וּמְקַיֵּם מַאֲמָרוֹ:

For trees blossoming:
Blessed are You, Source of all Life, whose world lacks nothing, creating goodly trees for our enjoyment.

בָּרוּךְ אַתָּה יהוה אֱלֹהֵינוּ מֶלֶךְ הָעוֹלָם.
שֶׁלֹּא חִסַּר בְּעוֹלָמוֹ דָּבָר. וּבָרָא בוֹ בְּרִיּוֹת
טוֹבוֹת וְאִילָנוֹת טוֹבִים לְהַנּוֹת בָּהֶם בְּנֵי
אָדָם:

For good news:
Blessed are You, Source of all Life, being good and doing good.

בָּרוּךְ אַתָּה יהוה אֱלֹהֵינוּ מֶלֶךְ הָעוֹלָם
הַטּוֹב וְהַמֵּטִיב:

For bad news:
Blessed are You, Source of all Life, being the true judge.

בָּרוּךְ אַתָּה יהוה אֱלֹהֵינוּ מֶלֶךְ הָעוֹלָם.
דַּיָּן הָאֱמֶת:

For travel:
May it be Your will, Eternal God, to guide me in peace and direct my steps so as to keep me safe from all dangers along the way, and bring blessing to the work of my hands, and to bring me home in peace.

יְהִי רָצוֹן מִלְּפָנֶיךָ יהוה אֱלֹהַי שֶׁתּוֹלִיכֵנִי
לְשָׁלוֹם וְתַצְעִידֵנִי לְשָׁלוֹם וְתַצִּילֵנִי
מִכָּל־סַכָּנָה בַּדֶּרֶךְ: וְתִשְׁלַח בְּרָכָה
בְּמַעֲשֵׂי יָדַי וּתְבִיאֵנִי בְשָׁלוֹם אֶל בֵּיתִי

The Eternal God shall guard your going out and your coming in, now and always.

יהוה יִשְׁמָר־צֵאתְךָ וּבוֹאֶךָ מֵעַתָּה וְעַד־
עוֹלָם

For a place where a wonderful thing happened to you:

Blessed are You, Source of all Life, performing a wonderful deed for me in this place.

For morning:

Blessed are You, Source of all Life, who has fashioned our bodies with wisdom, creating openings, arteries, glands and organs, wonderful in structure, intricate in design. Should but one of them, by being blocked or opened, fail to function, it would be difficult to stand before You. Wondrous fashioner and sustainer of life, Source of our health and our strength, we give You thanks and praise.

Blessed are You, Source of all Life, making me in the divine image.
Blessed are You, Source of all Life, leading me to my Jewish heritage.
Blessed are You, Source of all Life, making me free.

Blessed are You, Source of all Life, opening the eyes of those who cannot see.
Blessed are You, Source of all Life, providing clothes for the naked.
Blessed are You, Source of all Life, freeing the captive.
Blessed are You, Source of all Life, lifting up the downtrodden.
Blessed are You, Source of all Life, making firm each person's steps.
Blessed are You, Source of all Life, giving strength to the weary.

בָּרוּךְ אַתָּה יהוה אֱלֹהֵינוּ מֶלֶךְ הָעוֹלָם.
שֶׁעָשָׂה לִי נֵס בַּמָּקוֹם הַזֶּה

בָּרוּךְ אַתָּה יהוה אֱלֹהֵינוּ מֶלֶךְ הָעוֹלָם.
אֲשֶׁר יָצַר אֶת־הָאָדָם בְּחָכְמָה וּבָרָא בוֹ
נְקָבִים נְקָבִים חֲלוּלִים חֲלוּלִים גָּלוּי
וְיָדוּעַ לִפְנֵי כִסֵּא כְבוֹדֶךָ שֶׁאִם יִפָּתַח
אֶחָד מֵהֶם אוֹ יִסָּתֵם אֶחָד מֵהֶם אִי
אֶפְשָׁר לְהִתְקַיֵּם וְלַעֲמוֹד לְפָנֶיךָ בָּרוּךְ
אַתָּה יהוה רוֹפֵא כָל־בָּשָׂר וּמַפְלִיא
לַעֲשׂוֹת

בָּרוּךְ אַתָּה יהוה אֱלֹהֵינוּ
מֶלֶךְ הָעוֹלָם. שֶׁעָשַׂנִי בְּצַלְמוֹ:
בָּרוּךְ אַתָּה יהוה אֱלֹהֵינוּ
מֶלֶךְ הָעוֹלָם. שֶׁעָשַׂנִי יִשְׂרָאֵל:
בָּרוּךְ אַתָּה יהוה אֱלֹהֵינוּ מֶלֶךְ
הָעוֹלָם. שֶׁעָשַׂנִי בֶּן/בַּת חוֹרִין:

בָּרוּךְ אַתָּה יהוה אֱלֹהֵינוּ
מֶלֶךְ הָעוֹלָם. פּוֹקֵחַ עִוְרִים:
בָּרוּךְ אַתָּה יהוה אֱלֹהֵינוּ מֶלֶךְ
הָעוֹלָם. מַלְבִּישׁ עֲרֻמִּים:
בָּרוּךְ אַתָּה יהוה אֱלֹהֵינוּ מֶלֶךְ
הָעוֹלָם. מַתִּיר אֲסוּרִים:
בָּרוּךְ אַתָּה יהוה אֱלֹהֵינוּ מֶלֶךְ
הָעוֹלָם. זוֹקֵף כְּפוּפִים:
בָּרוּךְ אַתָּה יהוה אֱלֹהֵינוּ מֶלֶךְ
הָעוֹלָם. הַמֵּכִין מִצְעֲדֵי גָבֶר:
בָּרוּךְ אַתָּה יהוה אֱלֹהֵינוּ מֶלֶךְ
הָעוֹלָם. הַנּוֹתֵן לַיָּעֵף כֹּחַ:

58

For night-time:

Blessed are You, Source of all Life, closing my eyes in sleep. May it be Your will, Eternal God, that I lie down in peace and rise up in peace. Let not my thoughts or dreams upset me. Grant my family peace.

Grant me enlightenment, for You give light to the eyes. Blessed are You, Source of all Life, giving light to the world in all its glory.

Into Your hand, I place my soul
When I sleep; and when I wake
With my soul and body, God is with me,
I shall not fear.
(*Adon Olam*)

בָּרוּךְ אַתָּה יהוה אֱלֹהֵינוּ מֶלֶךְ הָעוֹלָם.
הַמַּפִּיל חֶבְלֵי שֵׁנָה עַל עֵינָי וּתְנוּמָה
עַל עַפְעַפָּי: וִיהִי רָצוֹן מִלְפָנֶיךָ יהוה
אֱלֹהַי וֵאלֹהֵי אֲבוֹתַי שֶׁתַּשְׁכִּיבֵנִי
לְשָׁלוֹם וְתַעֲמִידֵנִי לְשָׁלוֹם:
וְאַל יְבַהֲלוּנִי רַעְיוֹנַי וַחֲלוֹמוֹת רָעִים
וְהִרְהוֹרִים רָעִים:
וּתְהִי מִטָּתִי שְׁלֵמָה לְפָנֶיךָ בָּרוּךְ אַתָּה
יהוה הַמֵּאִיר לָעוֹלָם כֻּלּוֹ בִּכְבוֹדוֹ:

בְּיָדוֹ אַפְקִיד רוּחִי. בְּעֵת אִישַׁן
וְאָעִירָה: וְעִם רוּחִי גְּוִיָּתִי.
יהוה לִי וְלֹא אִירָא:

Mitzvot include a myriad of commandments and opportunities enjoined upon Jews to mark their daily lives. The actions which are performed may have either a ritual or an ethical purpose.

Chanukkat Habayit and for affixing the mezuzah (*the ceremony of dedicating a new home or building; a mezuzah is a handwritten parchment which includes the Shema prayer (see page 71) and the Ten Commandments, and which is placed in a holder on the doorposts of a house*):

Unless God builds the house, its builders work in vain.
(*Psalm 127:1*)

אִם־יְהֹוָה לֹא־יִבְנֶה בַיִת שָׁוְא עָמְלוּ בוֹנָיו בּוֹ:

Blessed are You, Source of all Life, making us holy through Your Commandments and commanding us to affix the mezuzah.

בָּרוּךְ אַתָּה יהוה אֱלֹהֵינוּ מֶלֶךְ הָעוֹלָם. אֲשֶׁר קִדְּשָׁנוּ בְּמִצְוֹתָיו וְצִוָּנוּ לִקְבּעַ מְזוּזָה:

You shall love the Eternal, your God, with all your heart and all your soul and all your might. These are the words which I entrust to your heart. Teach them faithfully to your children, speak of them in your home and outside of it, when you lie down and when you rise up. Seal them as a sign upon your hand and a symbol before your eyes, inscribe them on the doorposts of your house and upon your gates.
(*Deuteronomy, 6:5–9*)

וְאָהַבְתָּ אֵת יהוה אֱלֹהֶיךָ בְּכָל־לְבָבְךָ וּבְכָל־נַפְשְׁךָ וּבְכָל־מְאֹדֶךָ: וְהָיוּ הַדְּבָרִים הָאֵלֶּה אֲשֶׁר אָנֹכִי מְצַוְּךָ הַיּוֹם עַל־לְבָבֶךָ: וְשִׁנַּנְתָּם לְבָנֶיךָ וְדִבַּרְתָּ בָּם בְּשִׁבְתְּךָ בְּבֵיתֶךָ וּבְלֶכְתְּךָ בַדֶּרֶךְ וּבְשָׁכְבְּךָ וּבְקוּמֶךָ: וּקְשַׁרְתָּם לְאוֹת עַל־יָדֶךָ וְהָיוּ לְטֹטָפֹת בֵּין עֵינֶיךָ וּכְתַבְתָּם עַל־מְזֻזוֹת בֵּיתֶךָ וּבִשְׁעָרֶיךָ:

May God watch over you in your coming and going, now and always. Amen.

יהוה יִשְׁמָר צֵאתְךָ וּבוֹאֶךָ מֵעַתָּה וְעַד עוֹלָם. אָמֵן:

For construction on the home:
Blessed are You, Source of all Life, making us

בָּרוּךְ אַתָּה יהוה אֱלֹהֵינוּ מֶלֶךְ הָעוֹלָם.

holy through Your Commandments and commanding us to make our home safe.

For putting on a tallit (*a fringed shawl worn for prayer*):

Bless my soul, O God. You are very great, clothed in majesty and glory, wrapped in light like a gown. You spread out the heavens like a tent. I am about to wrap myself in this tallit to fulfil the commandment of my Creator. As it is written in the Torah: Each generation shall put fringes on the corners of their clothes. Just as I cover myself with a tallit in this world, so may my soul be dressed in a beautiful robe in the time to come. Amen.

Blessed are You, Source of all Life, making us holy through Your Commandments and commanding us to wrap ourselves in the tallit.

For laying tefillin (*a set of leather boxes worn on the arm and head as a daily reminder of God's teachings*):

On the arm:

Blessed are You, Source of all Life, making us holy through Your Commandments and commanding us to lay tefillin.

On the head:

Blessed are You, Source of all Life, making us holy through Your Commandments and commanding us concerning tefillin.

אֲשֶׁר קִדְּשָׁנוּ בְּמִצְוֹתָיו וְצִוָּנוּ לַעֲשׂוֹת מַעֲקֶה:

בָּרְכִי נַפְשִׁי אֶת־יהוה יהוה אֱלֹהַי גָּדַלְתָּ מְּאֹד הוֹד וְהָדָר לָבָשְׁתָּ: עֹטֶה־אוֹר כַּשַּׂלְמָה נוֹטֶה שָׁמַיִם כַּיְרִיעָה: הִנְנִי מִתְעַטֵּף בְּטַלִּית שֶׁל־צִיצִת כְּדֵי לְקַיֵּם מִצְוַת בּוֹרְאִי. כַּכָּתוּב בַּתּוֹרָה. וְעָשׂוּ לָהֶם צִיצִת עַל־כַּנְפֵי בִגְדֵיהֶם לְדֹרֹתָם. וּכְשֵׁם שֶׁאֲנִי מִתְכַּסֶּה בְּטַלִּית בָּעוֹלָם הַזֶּה כֵּן תִּזְכֶּה נִשְׁמָתִי לְהִתְלַבֵּשׁ בְּטַלִּית נָאָה לָעוֹלָם הַבָּא בְּגַן עֵדֶן. אָמֵן:

בָּרוּךְ אַתָּה יהוה אֱלֹהֵינוּ מֶלֶךְ הָעוֹלָם. אֲשֶׁר קִדְּשָׁנוּ בְּמִצְוֹתָיו וְצִוָּנוּ לְהִתְעַטֵּף בַּצִּיצִת:

בָּרוּךְ אַתָּה יהוה אֱלֹהֵינוּ מֶלֶךְ הָעוֹלָם. אֲשֶׁר קִדְּשָׁנוּ בְּמִצְוֹתָיו וְצִוָּנוּ לְהָנִיחַ תְּפִלִּין:

בָּרוּךְ אַתָּה יהוה אֱלֹהֵינוּ מֶלֶךְ הָעוֹלָם. אֲשֶׁר קִדְּשָׁנוּ בְּמִצְוֹתָיו וְצִוָּנוּ עַל־מִצְוַת תְּפִלִּין:

Blessed is God's name for ever.

I will betroth you to me forever.
I will betroth you to me in righteousness
and justice, in love and compassion.
I will betroth you to me in faithfulness
and so you will know God.
(*Hosea, 2:21–22*)

For acts of kindness:
Blessed are You, Source of all Life,
making us holy through Your
Commandments and commanding us to
carry out loving deeds.

בָּרוּךְ שֵׁם כְּבוֹד מַלְכוּתוֹ לְעוֹלָם וָעֶד:

וְאֵרַשְׂתִּיךְ לִי לְעוֹלָם
וְאֵרַשְׂתִּיךְ לִי בְּצֶדֶק
וּבְמִשְׁפָּט וּבְחֶסֶד וּבְרַחֲמִים:
וְאֵרַשְׂתִּיךְ לִי בֶּאֱמוּנָה
וְיָדַעַתְּ אֶת־יהוה:

בָּרוּךְ אַתָּה יהוה אֱלֹהֵינוּ מֶלֶךְ
הָעוֹלָם. אֲשֶׁר קִדְּשָׁנוּ בְּמִצְוֹתָיו וְצִוָּנוּ
עַל גְּמִילוּת חֲסָדִים:

For hope:
Have hope in the Eternal One,
Be strong and your heart will be
strengthened,
Have hope in God.
(*Psalm 27:14*)

קַוֵּה אֶל־יהוה חֲזַק וְיַאֲמֵץ
לִבֶּךָ וְקַוֵּה אֶל־יהוה:

I lift up my eyes to the hills,
Where will my help come from?
My help comes from God,
Creator of heaven and earth.
(*Psalm 121:1–2*)

אֶשָּׂא עֵינַי אֶל־הֶהָרִים מֵאַיִן
יָבֹא עֶזְרִי: עֶזְרִי מֵעִם יהוה
עֹשֵׂה שָׁמַיִם וָאָרֶץ:

In times of fear:
The entire world is a very narrow bridge,
And the essential thing is not to be
afraid.
(*Likutei Maharan, 2:28*)

כָּל־הָעוֹלָם כֻּלּוֹ
גֶּשֶׁר צַר מְאֹד
וְהָעִקָּר לֹא לְפַחֵד כְּלָל:

In times of sorrow:
O God, You have searched me
And know me well,
You understand all my thoughts,
And every word upon my tongue,
Your presence surrounds me,
If I say: Let darkness hide me, and turn
the light to darkness, even the darkness
is not dark for You. The night shines
forth like day,
The darkness is as light to You.
Search my soul, O God, and know
my heart.
If there is sorrow in me,
Lead me in Your everlasting ways.
(*Psalm 139:1–5, 11–12, 23–24*)

יְהוָֹה חֲקַרְתַּנִי וַתֵּדָע:
אַתָּה יָדַעְתָּ שִׁבְתִּי וְקוּמִי בַּנְתָּה לְרֵעִי
מֵרָחוֹק:
אָרְחִי וְרִבְעִי זֵרִיתָ וְכָל־דְּרָכַי
הִסְכַּנְתָּה:
כִּי אֵין מִלָּה בִּלְשׁוֹנִי הֵן יְהוָֹה יָדַעְתָּ
כֻלָּהּ:
אָחוֹר וָקֶדֶם צַרְתָּנִי
וַתָּשֶׁת עָלַי כַּפֶּכָה:
וָאֹמַר אַךְ־חֹשֶׁךְ יְשׁוּפֵנִי וְלַיְלָה אוֹר
בַּעֲדֵנִי:
גַּם־חֹשֶׁךְ לֹא־יַחְשִׁיךְ מִמֶּךָ וְלַיְלָה כַּיּוֹם
יָאִיר כַּחֲשֵׁיכָה כָּאוֹרָה:
חָקְרֵנִי אֵל וְדַע לְבָבִי בְּחָנֵנִי וְדַע
שַׂרְעַפָּי:
וּרְאֵה אִם־דֶּרֶךְ־עֹצֶב בִּי וּנְחֵנִי בְּדֶרֶךְ
עוֹלָם:

For dreaming:

If you have seen a dream and do not remember what you saw, stand before the Priests at the time of the priestly benediction and say as follows: Sovereign of the Universe, I am Yours and my dreams are Yours. I have dreamed a dream and I do not know what it is. Whether I have dreamed about myself, my companions have dreamed about me, or I have dreamed about others, if they are good dreams, affirm them. May they be fulfilled like the dreams of Joseph. If they require healing, heal them as the waters of Marah were healed by Moses, and Miriam was healed of her leprosy. As You turned the curse of Balaam into a blessing, so turn all my dreams into something good for me.
(*Talmud Berachot, 55b*)

הַאי מַאן דַּחֲזָא חֶלְמָא וְלָא יָדַע מַאי חֲזָא
לֵיקוּם קַמֵּי כָּהֲנֵי בְּעִידָנָא דְּפָרְסֵי יְדַיְיהוּ
וְלֵימָא הָכִי רִבּוֹנוֹ שֶׁל עוֹלָם אֲנִי שֶׁלָּךְ
וַחֲלוֹמוֹתַי שֶׁלָּךְ חֲלוֹם חָלַמְתִּי וְאֵינִי יוֹדֵעַ
מַה הוּא בֵּין שֶׁחָלַמְתִּי אֲנִי לְעַצְמִי וּבֵין
שֶׁחָלְמוּ לִי חֲבֵירַי וּבֵין שֶׁחָלַמְתִּי עַל
אֲחֵרִים אִם טוֹבִים הֵם חַזְּקֵם וְאַמְּצֵם
כַּחֲלוֹמוֹתָיו שֶׁל יוֹסֵף וְאִם צְרִיכִים
רְפוּאָה רְפָאֵם כְּמֵי מָרָה עַל יְדֵי מֹשֶׁה
רַבֵּינוּ וּכְמִרְיָם מִצָּרַעְתָּהּ וּכְחִזְקִיָּה מֵחָלְיוֹ
וּכְמֵי יְרִיחוֹ עַל יְדֵי אֱלִישָׁע וּכְשֵׁם
שֶׁהָפַכְתָּ קִלְלַת בִּלְעָם הָרָשָׁע לִבְרָכָה כֵּן
הֲפוֹךְ כָּל חֲלוֹמוֹתַי עָלַי לְטוֹבָה וּמְסַיֵּים
בַּהֲדֵי כָהֲנֵי דְּעָנֵי צִבּוּרָא

For wisdom:

Rabbi Ben Zoma used to say: Who is wise?
One who learns from every person.
For we learn: From all my teachers I have gained understanding.
(*Pirkei Avot, 4:1*)

בֶּן זוֹמָא אוֹמֵר:
אֵיזֶהוּ חָכָם? הַלּוֹמֵד מִכָּל
אָדָם, שֶׁנֶּאֱמַר:
מִכָּל מְלַמְּדַי הִשְׂכַּלְתִּי.

Rabbi Eleazar ben Azariah used to say:
Without Torah, there is no respect.
Without respect, there can be no Torah.
Without wisdom, there is no reverence.
Without reverence, there can be no Torah.
Without discernment, there is no knowledge.
Without knowledge, there can be no discernment.
Without a livelihood, there is no Torah,
Without Torah, there can be no livelihood.
(*Pirkei Avot, 3:21*)

רַבִּי אֶלְעָזָר בֶּן עֲזַרְיָה אוֹמֵר:
אִם אֵין תּוֹרָה אֵין דֶּרֶךְ אֶרֶץ;
אִם אֵין דֶּרֶךְ אֶרֶץ, אֵין תּוֹרָה.
אִם אֵין חָכְמָה, אֵין יִרְאָה;
אִם אֵין יִרְאָה, אֵין חָכְמָה.
אִם אֵין בִּינָה, אֵין דַּעַת;
אִם אֵין דַּעַת, אֵין בִּינָה.
אִם אֵין קֶמַח, אֵין תּוֹרָה;
אִם אֵין תּוֹרָה, אֵין קֶמַח.

One who has more learning than good deeds is like a tree with many branches but few roots; when the wind comes, it uproots the tree and topples it. But one who has more good deeds than learning is like a tree with few branches but many roots. Even if all the winds in the world were to come and blow against it, they wouldn't be able to move it from its place.

(*Pirkei Avot, 3:22*)

כָּל־שֶׁחָכְמָתוֹ מְרֻבָּה מִמַּעֲשָׂיו לְמָה הוּא דוֹמֶה? לְאִילָן שֶׁעֲנָפָיו מְרֻבִּין וְשָׁרָשָׁיו מֻעָטִין וְהָרוּחַ בָּאָה וְעוֹקַרְתּוּ וְהוֹפַכְתּוּ עַל פָּנָיו. אֲבָל כָּל־שֶׁמַּעֲשָׂיו מְרֻבִּין לְמָה הוּא דוֹמֶה? לְאִילָן שֶׁעֲנָפָיו מֻעָטִין וְשָׁרָשָׁיו מְרֻבִּין שֶׁאֲפִילוּ כָּל־הָרוּחוֹת שֶׁבָּעוֹלָם בָּאוֹת וְנוֹשְׁבוֹת בּוֹ אֵין מְזִיזוֹת אוֹתוֹ מִמְּקוֹמוֹ:

There are four kinds of deeds that bring benefit in this world but whose full reward is reserved for the world-to-come, and they are: respecting father and mother, performing deeds of loving kindness, bringing peace between one and another, and studying the Torah, which is equal to all of them.

(*Avot d'Rabbi Nathan, 40*)

אַרְבָּעָה דְבָרִים אָדָם עוֹשֶׂה אוֹתָן אוֹכֵל פֵּרוֹתֵיהֶן בָּעוֹלָם הַזֶּה וְהַקֶּרֶן קַיֶּמֶת לוֹ לָעוֹלָם הַבָּה וְאֵלּוּ הֵן כִּבּוּד אָב וָאֵם וּגְמִילוּת חֲסָדִים וַהֲבָאַת שָׁלוֹם בֵּין אָדָם לַחֲבֵרוֹ וְתַלְמוּד תּוֹרָה כְּנֶגֶד כֻּלָּם

For self or selflessness:

Hillel used to say: If I am not for myself, who will be for me?
And if I am only for myself, what am I?
And if not now, then when?

(*Pirkei Avot, 1:14*)

הִלֵּל הָיָה אוֹמֵר: אִם אֵין אֲנִי לִי, מִי לִי?
וּכְשֶׁאֲנִי לְעַצְמִי מָה אֲנִי?
וְאִם לֹא עַכְשָׁיו אֵימָתַי?

For companionship:

May it be Your will, Eternal God, that love and harmony, peace and friendship may dwell among us. Help us to look forward with confidence and hope. Guide us in the world with good companions and good intentions. When we rise in the morning, may we find our hearts ready to

יְהִי רָצוֹן מִלְּפָנֶיךָ יהוה אֱלֹהֵינוּ שֶׁתַּשְׁכֵּן בְּפוּרֵינוּ אַהֲבָה וְאַחֲוָה וְשָׁלוֹם וְרֵעוּת, וְתַרְבֶּה גְּבוּלֵנוּ בְּתַלְמִידִים, וְתַצְלִיחַ סוֹפֵינוּ אַחֲרִית וְתִקְוָה, וְתָשִׂים חֶלְקֵנוּ בְּגַן עֵדֶן, וְתַקְּנֵנוּ בְּחָבֵר טוֹב וְיֵצֶר טוֹב בְּעוֹלָמְךָ, וְנַשְׁכִּים וְנִמְצָא יָחוּל לְבָבֵנוּ לְיִרְאָה אֶת שְׁמֶךָ, וְתָבֹא

revere You, and may our deepest longings be fulfilled for our own good.
(*Talmud Berachot, 16b*)

לְפָנֶיךָ קוֹרַת נַפְשֵׁנוּ לְטוֹבָה.

For a good life:
Eternal God, grant us long life;
A life of peace,
A life of good,
A life of blessing,
A life of prosperity,
A life of health,
A life guided by fear of sin,
A life lived without shame,
A life rich and honest,
A life quickened by love of Torah and the fear of heaven,
A life in which our hearts' desires are fulfilled for our own good.
(*Talmud Berachot, 16b*)

יְהִי רָצוֹן מִלְּפָנֶיךָ יהוה
אֱלֹהֵינוּ שֶׁתִּתֶּן לָנוּ
חַיִּים אֲרוּכִים,
חַיִּים שֶׁל שָׁלוֹם,
חַיִּים שֶׁל טוֹבָה,
חַיִּים שֶׁל בְּרָכָה,
חַיִּים שֶׁל פַּרְנָסָה,
חַיִּים שֶׁל חִלּוּץ עֲצָמוֹת,
חַיִּים שֶׁיֵּשׁ בָּהֶם יִרְאַת חֵטְא,
חַיִּים שֶׁאֵין בָּהֶם בּוּשָׁה וּכְלִימָה,
חַיִּים שֶׁל עֹשֶׁר וְכָבוֹד,
חַיִּים שֶׁתְּהֵא בָנוּ אַהֲבַת תּוֹרָה וְיִרְאַת שָׁמַיִם,
חַיִּים שֶׁתְּמַלֵּא לָנוּ אֶת כָּל מִשְׁאֲלוֹת לִבֵּנוּ לְטוֹבָה.

For insight:
Don't look at a bottle, but at what is in it. There are new bottles full of old wine, and old ones that don't even contain new wine.
(*Pirkei Avot, 4:27*)

אַל־תִּסְתַּכֵּל בַּקַּנְקַן אֶלָּא בְּמַה שֶׁיֶּשׁ־בּוֹ:
יֵשׁ קַנְקַן חָדָשׁ מָלֵא יָשָׁן וְיָשָׁן שֶׁאֲפִילוּ חָדָשׁ אֵין בּוֹ:

For taking action:
All is foreseen yet free choice is given; the world is judged as good and all depends on the balance of the deeds.
(*Pirkei Avot, 3:19*)

הַכֹּל צָפוּי, וְהָרְשׁוּת נְתוּנָה; וּבְטוֹב הָעוֹלָם נִדּוֹן, וְהַכֹּל לְפִי רֹב הַמַּעֲשֶׂה.

For building a reputation:
There are three crowns: the crown of Torah, the crown of priesthood, and the

שְׁלֹשָׁה כְתָרִים הֵם: כֶּתֶר תּוֹרָה וְכֶתֶר כְּהֻנָּה וְכֶתֶר מַלְכוּת. וְכֶתֶר שֵׁם טוֹב

crown of royalty, but the crown of a good name exceeds them all.
(*Pirkei Avot, 4:17*)

עוֹלָה עַל גַּבֵּיהֶם.

For fate:

The world is like an anteroom to the world to come. Prepare yourself in the anteroom so that you may enter the hall. Better one hour of repentance and good deeds in this world, than a lifetime in the world to come.
(*Pirkei Avot, 4:16–17*)

הָעוֹלָם הַזֶּה דּוֹמֶה לַפְּרוֹזְדוֹר בִּפְנֵי הָעוֹלָם הַבָּא; הַתְקֵן עַצְמְךָ בַּפְּרוֹזְדוֹר כְּדֵי שֶׁתִּכָּנֵס לַטְּרַקְלִין. יָפָה שָׁעָה אַחַת בִּתְשׁוּבָה וּמַעֲשִׂים טוֹבִים בָּעוֹלָם הַזֶּה מִכָּל־חַיֵּי הָעוֹלָם הַבָּא.

For courage:

In places where there are no good people, be a good person.
(*Pirkei Avot, 2:5*)

וּבְמָקוֹם שֶׁאֵין אֲנָשִׁים, הִשְׁתַּדֵּל לִהְיוֹת אִישׁ.

For fulfilment:

You are not required to complete the task, but neither are you at liberty to abstain from it.
(*Pirkei Avot, 2:21*)

לֹא עָלֶיךָ הַמְּלָאכָה לִגְמוֹר וְלֹא אַתָּה בֶּן־חוֹרִין לְהִבָּטֵל מִמֶּנָּה.

If I am here, all are here.
If I am not here, who is here?
(*Avot d'Rabbi Nathan, 12*)

אִם אֲנִי כָּאן הַכֹּל כָּאן אִם אֲנִי לֵית כָּאן מָאן כָּאן

For friendship:

May the One whose presence dwells in this house cause love and harmony, peace and friendship to dwell among us.
(*Talmud Berachot, 12a*)

מִי שֶׁשָּׁכֵן אֶת־שְׁמוֹ בַּבַּיִת הַזֶּה הוּא יַשְׁכִּין בֵּינֵיכֶם אַהֲבָה וְאַחֲוָה וְשָׁלוֹם וְרֵעוּת

For God's love:

May God bless us with all good and

יְבָרֶכְכָה בְּכֹל טוֹב וְיִשְׁמוֹרְכָה מִכֹּל

keep us from all evil.

May God teach our hearts the meaning of life and grant us knowledge of the infinite.

May God reach out to us with tenderness so that we may have peace.

(*Dead Sea Scrolls*)

Our God and God of our ancestors, bless us with the threefold blessings of the Torah:

May God bless you and keep you.

May God look kindly upon you and be gracious to you.

May God reach out to you in tenderness and give you peace.

(*Numbers, 6:24–26*)

רַע
וְיָאִיר לְבָבְכָה בְּשֵׂכֶל חַיִּים וְיָחוֹנְכָה בְּדַעַת עוֹלָמִים
וְיִשָּׂא פְּנֵי חֲסָדָיו לְכָה לְשָׁלוֹם עוֹלָמִים

אֱלֹהֵינוּ וֵאלֹהֵי אֲבוֹתֵינוּ וְאִמּוֹתֵינוּ
בָּרְכֵנוּ בַּבְּרָכָה הַמְשֻׁלֶּשֶׁת הַכְּתוּבָה בַּתּוֹרָה:
יְבָרֶכְךָ יהוה וְיִשְׁמְרֶךָ: יָאֵר יהוה פָּנָיו אֵלֶיךָ וִיחֻנֶּךָּ: יִשָּׂא יהוה פָּנָיו אֵלֶיךָ וְיָשֵׂם לְךָ שָׁלוֹם:

PRAYERS FOR HEALING

תְּפִלּוֹת לִרְפוּאָה שְׁלֵמָה

For the sick:

May it be Your will, Source of all Life and God of our ancestors, to grant perfect healing, a healing of body and a healing of mind and soul to all those who are ill. Blessed are You, Source of all Life, healing the sick.

וִיהִי רָצוֹן מִלְּפָנֶיךָ יהוה אֱלֹהֵינוּ וֵאלֹהֵי אֲבוֹתֵינוּ וְאִמּוֹתֵינוּ שֶׁתִּשְׁלַח מְהֵרָה רְפוּאָה שְׁלֵמָה רְפוּאַת הַנֶּפֶשׁ וּרְפוּאַת הַגּוּף בְּתוֹךְ שְׁאָר הַחוֹלִים בָּרוּךְ אַתָּה יהוה רוֹפֵא הַחוֹלִים:

For the healing power of others:

Rabbi Hiyya fell ill.
Rabbi Yohanan went to visit him.
Rabbi Yohanan asked: 'Do you want to be sick? Is your suffering important to you?'
When Rabbi Hiyya answered: 'No,' Rabbi Yohanan placed his hands on him and healed him.
Then this same Rabbi Yohanan fell ill.
Rabbi Hanina went to visit him and asked:
'Is your suffering important to you?'
Rabbi Yohanan said: 'No,' and Rabbi Hanina placed his hands upon him and healed him.
If Rabbi Yohanan could heal Rabbi Hiyya, why, then, when Rabbi Yohanan got sick, could he not heal himself?
Prisoners cannot release themselves from their own confinement.
(*Talmud Berachot, 5b*)

רַבִּי חִיָּיא בַּר אַבָּא חֲלַשׁ,
עַל לְגַבֵּיהּ רַבִּי יוֹחָנָן אֲמַר לֵיהּ:
חֲבִיבִין עֲלֵיךְ יִסּוּרִין? אֲמַר לֵיהּ:
לֹא הֵן וְלֹא שְׂכָרָן. אֲמַר לֵיהּ:
הַב לִי יָדְךָ! יְהַב לֵיהּ יְדֵיהּ
וְאוֹקְמֵיהּ. רַבִּי יוֹחָנָן חֲלַשׁ עַל
לְגַבֵּיהּ רַבִּי חֲנִינָא. אֲמַר
לֵיהּ: חֲבִיבִין עֲלֵיךְ יִסּוּרִין?
אֲמַר לֵיהּ: לֹא הֵן וְלֹא שְׂכָרָן.
אֲמַר לֵיהּ: הַב לִי יָדְךָ! יְהַב לֵיהּ
יְדֵיהּ וְאוֹקְמֵיהּ. אַמַּאי? לוֹקִים
רַבִּי יוֹחָנָן לְנַפְשֵׁיהּ! – אָמְרִי: אֵין
חָבוּשׁ מַתִּיר עַצְמוֹ
מִבֵּית הָאֲסוּרִים.

For self-healing:

Heal me, O God, and I shall be healed;
Save me and I shall be saved;
For You are my consolation.
Blessed are You, God, healing the sick.

רְפָאֵנִי יהוה וְאֵרָפֵא
הוֹשִׁיעֵנִי וְאִוָּשֵׁעָה.
כִּי תְהִלָּתִי אָתָּה.
בָּרוּךְ אַתָּה יהוה. רוֹפֵה
הַחוֹלִים:

Before an operation:
Into Your hand I place my soul,
Both when I sleep and when I wake,
With my spirit and my body,
You are with me, I shall not fear.
(*Adon Olam*)

בְּיָדוֹ אַפְקִיד רוּחִי.
בְּעֵת אִישָׁן וְאָעִירָה:
וְעִם רוּחִי גְוִיָּתִי.
יהוה לִי וְלֹא אִירָא:

For recuperation:
Blessed are You, Source of all Life, showing
goodness to me as to all others.

בָּרוּךְ אַתָּה יהוה אֱלֹהֵינוּ מֶלֶךְ הָעוֹלָם.
הַגּוֹמֵל לְחַיָּבִים:

For the affirmation of faith (*traditionally
called the* Shema *prayer*):
Hear, O Israel!
The Eternal is our God, the Eternal is One.
Praised be the name of God, whose glorious
rule is for ever and ever.
Love the Eternal, your God, with all your
heart, and with all your soul and with all
your might.
These words, that I command you today,
shall be on your heart: Impress them on
your children, talk about them when sitting
in your home, and when going on your way,
and when you lie down and when you get up.
Bind them as a sign on your hand, and they
shall be reminders between your eyes.
Write them on the doorposts of your house,
and on your gates.

שְׁמַע יִשְׂרָאֵל
יהוה אֱלֹהֵינוּ יהוה אֶחָד:
בָּרוּךְ שֵׁם כְּבוֹד מַלְכוּתוֹ לְעוֹלָם וָעֶד:
וְאָהַבְתָּ אֵת יהוה אֱלֹהֶיךָ בְּכָל־לְבָבְךָ
וּבְכָל־נַפְשְׁךָ וּבְכָל־מְאֹדֶךָ: וְהָיוּ
הַדְּבָרִים הָאֵלֶּה אֲשֶׁר אָנֹכִי מְצַוְּךָ
הַיּוֹם עַל־לְבָבֶךָ: וְשִׁנַּנְתָּם לְבָנֶיךָ
וְדִבַּרְתָּ בָּם בְּשִׁבְתְּךָ בְּבֵיתֶךָ וּבְלֶכְתְּךָ
בַדֶּרֶךְ וּבְשָׁכְבְּךָ וּבְקוּמֶךָ: וּקְשַׁרְתָּם
לְאוֹת עַל־יָדֶךָ וְהָיוּ לְטֹטָפֹת בֵּין
עֵינֶיךָ: וּכְתַבְתָּם עַל מְזֻזוֹת בֵּיתֶךָ
וּבִשְׁעָרֶיךָ:

INDEX OF BLESSINGS

DETAILS OF MANUSCRIPTS

Manuscripts from the Bodleian Library

Catalan Maimonides: Moreh Nevukhim (*Sephardi*)

MS. Laud. Or. 234, Catalonia, c. 1350, vellum

The Guide to the Perplexed in Shmuel ibn Tibbon's Hebrew translation, preceded by an index of passages from the Pentateuch and by the chapter index. Marginal notes in two hands chiefly contain omissions. At the beginning is a letter addressed to rabbinical colleagues by Mosheh Bonyaq Botarel. A note names the owner as Reuven ben Yehudah Hasdai, stating that he pawned the manuscript to Don Zerahyah ben Gwiosnero for one hundred dinars, at Huesca, on Wednesday 26th Iyyar 1356. The Spanish illumination shows some French and Italianate features such as very delicate coloring, although the forms are rigid and angular.

First Kennicott Bible (*Sephardi*)

MS. Kennicott I, northwest Spain, 1476, vellum

Pentateuch together with D. Kimhi's grammatical treatise *Mikhlol*. The manuscript is recognized as a masterpiece of late Sephardic illumination. The text, in splendid Spanish square characters, was written by the scribe Moses ibn Zabarah. The artist of the sumptuous illuminations was Joseph ibn Hayyim. The work is dated 1476 and attributed to the city of La Coruña.

The color scheme is bright and lively, with rhythmic repetition of patterns and motifs. The filigree penwork shows the scribe as conscious of visual effect as the artist. Contemporary themes in the manuscript's decoration include playing cards, zoomorphic and anthropomorphic letters, and the influence of French, Italian and Flemish illumination. Prime features of the work include panel pages, magnificent 'carpet' pages and the arcading surrounding the *Mikhlol*. The carpet pages, which feature complex interlacing bands and elements drawn from mosaic floors and the Temple *Torah* niche, display influence from the Coptic and northern gospels as well as from Islam. Suggesting schematic plans of the Temple, these pages symbolically evoke hope of redemption.

Liturgy (*Ashkenazi*)

MS. Opp. 776, Germany, 1471, vellum

Prayers, beginning with *Mah tovu* and *Adon*, followed by *Avot* and *Hosh'anah*. This manuscript was written by Asher ben Yishaq ha-Shoa and finished in 1471. Neubauer describes the illustrations as 'common illuminations'; in fact, as the lions pictured here (page 19) show, the illuminations are lively and expressive as well as colorful and skillfully executed. Though not specifically related to details of the text, they evoke the general idea of prayer and praise.

Machzor (*Ashkenazi*)

MS. Laud. Or. 321, Germany, c. 1275, vellum

The prayerbook of the Western Ashkenazi rite, with some liturgies from the Eastern Ashkenazi, beginning with *parshiyot* for various Sabbaths and feasts, followed by *Canticles, Ruth,*

Ecclesiastes and the *Haftaroth*. There are marginal notes in two hands. The owner is named as Yehudah ha-Mekhuneh.

Pentateuch (*Ashkenazi*)

MS. Canon. Or. 62, northern Italy, 1472, vellum

The manuscript also contains *Esther, Song of Songs, Ruth, Lamentations, Ecclesiastes* and *Haftaroth*, with commentaries by Ibn Ezra, Rashi and Abraham Levi. It was written in Italy by Berakhiel ben Hizqiyah Rephael Trabot and was finished in 1472. In some places the marginal commentary by Rashi is written in the form of the letters of 'Abram Rabba', the patron's name. There are good illuminations at the beginning of each book. The unusually shaped initial word letters make it likely that the illuminator was a non-Jew, as does the use in *Genesis* 2:6 of the stag, the virgin and the unicorn, figures which have no significance in Jewish illumination and which, along with the figures of Adam, Eve and the serpent are suggestive of Italian illumination of the Ferrara School.

Tur Even ha-Ezer and Tur Hoshen ha-Mishpat (*Sephardi*)

MS. Canon. Or. 79, Italy, 1438, vellum

Codes of Jewish law by Jacob ben Asher (1269–1340). The manuscript was written by Mosheh Beth-El from Avignon and finished in 1438. The name of the person for whom the manuscript was written has been erased. This is probably an Italian manuscript, written in Sephardi rabbinic semi-cursive characters, with illuminations. At the beginning of each section is an index and the Arabic or Spanish explanations of difficult words used.

Manuscripts from the British Library

Bible (*Ashkenazi*)

MS. Add. 11657, Germany, probably fourteenth century, vellum

This biblical codex written in beautiful Ashkenazi square script contains only the books of the Former and Latter Prophets. The scribe Meshullam signed his name in red ink in *Kings*. The opening pages to *Joshua* and *Isaiah* are richly illuminated with painted designs enhanced with gold. The first pages of the other books in the manuscript are marked with ornate initial word panels and beautifully painted borders.

French Miscellany (*Ashkenazi*)

MS. Add. 11639, northern France, c. 1280, vellum

One of the finest extant French Hebrew manuscripts, it was written by a scribe named Benjamin and comprises a variety of · biblical, liturgical and historical texts. Several artists were responsible for the exquisite decorations, ranging from elaborate borders with animal, floral and grotesque motifs to full-page miniatures, some circular in shape, displaying the sophistication of French Gothic manuscript art. The whole-page illuminations are biblical, midrashic and messianic in scope, but bear no relevance to the texts and may have been added later. Although the colophon is absent, specific inclusions, such as a calendar for the new moon 1280–96 and the *Sefer Mitsvot Katan* (Small Book of Commandments) written by Isaac of Corbeil in about 1276, set the date of the *French Miscellany* close to 1280.

German Machzor (*Ashkenazi*)
MS. Add. 22413, southern Germany, c. 1320, vellum
Festival prayers for *Shavuot* and *Sukkot*, according to the German rite, with commentaries, copied by Hayim. A pupil of Rabbi Meir of Rothenburg, Hayim was apparently a prolific scribe active in southern Germany. The seven miniatures in the codex, some of which show animal-headed characters, were probably the work of another artist. This manuscript forms part two of the *Tripartite Machzor*, a festival prayer book in three parts. Parts one and three are held at the Library of the Hungarian Academy of Sciences, Budapest, and in the Bodleian Library, Oxford, respectively.

Golden Haggadah (*Sephardi*)
MS. Add. 27210, northern Spain (probably Barcelona), c. 1320, vellum
A Sephardi *Haggadah* whose fame is attributed to the gold leaf variegated background of the full-page biblical illuminations at the beginning of the manuscript. The middle and last sections contain the *Haggadah* text and Passover liturgical poems – *piyutim* – according to the Sephardi rite. The elegant miniatures, based mainly on episodes from *Genesis*, *Exodus* and the *Midrash*, were produced by two artists in the French Gothic style but, through lack of a colophon, their identities remain unknown. The *Golden Haggadah* was probably brought to Italy in around 1492, by Jews fleeing Spain. In 1602 in Carpi, near Modena, Rabbi Joav Gallico presented it as a wedding gift to his daughter and son-in-law. The *Golden Haggadah*'s last known owner was the nineteenth-century poet and bibliophile Joseph Almanzi.

Italian Machzor (*Italian Rite*)
MS. Add.16577, Italy, fifteenth century, vellum
Festival prayers according to the Roman rite. The manuscript comprises finely illuminated pages showing the influence of Renaissance art. The elaborate borders painted with fleshy scrolls and floral designs interspersed with animals, vases and gold dots are particularly handsome. An array of word panels outlined in vibrant hues of pink, green and blue embellished with golden buds and multicolored vegetal motifs, enhance the aesthetic quality of the manuscript. Abraham ben Jacob, most likely its first owner, inscribed his name on the profusely illuminated last page of the codex.

Italian Machzor (*Italian Rite*)
MS. Harley 5686, Italy, 1466, vellum
Manuscript containing festival prayers, as well as a series of miscellaneous texts written in the margins. There are two colophons in this codex. The main body of the manuscript was copied around 1466 by Leon ben Joshua de Rossi of Cesena for a patron named Joab Immanuel. The section on *Tahanunim* (Supplications), dated 1427, may have originally been a separate manuscript and was completed at Bologna by Isaac ben Obadiah David of Forli for Joseph ben Solomon Kohen. A number of textual illustrations painted in rich color complement some of the main sections in the manuscript.

Legal Decisions
MS. Or. 5024, Italy, 1374, vellum
Halakhic decisions of Isaiah ben Elijah of Trani, the Younger, copied by Jekuthiel ben Solomon for his teacher Menahem ben Nathan. The codex abounds in finely illuminated borders, word panels and textual illustrations executed in rich shades of pink, green, red and brilliant blue (the predominant hue). It is a good example of Hebrew legal text decoration in Italy during the period. The practice of decorating Latin legal codes originated in thirteenth-century Bologna. According to Joseph Gutmann, the illuminations in this manuscript were probably executed in the workshop of Nicollo di Giacomo da Bologna.

Leipnik Haggadah (*Ashkenazi*)
MS. Sloane 3173, Altona, 1740, vellum
The Passover night ritual with commentary by Isaac Abarbanel, copied and illuminated by Joseph ben David of Leipnik, an influential Moravian scribe-artist active in Hamburg and Altona who, between 1731 and 1740, produced some thirteen *Haggadot*. As in other *Haggadah* manuscripts of the time, the illuminations in this manuscript were modeled on the engravings in the 1695 and 1712 printed editions of the *Amsterdam Haggadah*. This beautiful manuscript belonged to Sir Hans Sloane (1660–1753), one of the founders of the British Museum.

Liturgical Selections (*Ashkenazi*)
MS. Harley 5713, England, 1714, vellum
Manuscript containing Sabbath prayers, blessings for festivals and special occasions, and the Hebrew versions of *Tobit* and *Antiochus*. The scribe, Aaron ben Moses, exhibits a fine hand in the square Ashkenazi style of writing. It is possible that the unusual, color pen illustrations were created by a different artist. The aristocratic provenance of the codex is indicated on its frontispiece: it was commissioned by Humphrey Wanley, librarian of Robert Harley, First Earl of Oxford (1661–1724).

Sister Haggadah (*Sephardi*)
MS. Or. 2884, northern Spain (probably Barcelona), mid-fourteenth century, vellum
This manuscript shares common traits with the *Golden Haggadah*, hence its name. Apart from the similarities of layout and iconography, scholars believe that the artists of both *Haggadot* probably based their work on a common model. The creators of the *Sister Haggadah*, however, show lesser skill in their artistry.

(front and back endpapers) Bod. MS. Canon. Or. 62, f.240v (detail) (*Pentateuch*)
One of the many intricate designs framing the first word of a *parashah* (the part of a text that is read in the synagogue).

(p.5) BL MS. Or. 5024, f.85r (*Legal Decisions*)
A man watering his garden illustrates *Piske Mashkin* – the laws concerning irrigation and other activities restricted between the festivals of Passover and *Sukkot*. The charm of this illustration lies in the detailed depiction of the vegetation, in the person's finely drawn profile and in the vibrant blue lapis lazuli coloring of his gown and headgear.

(p.7) BL MS. Add. 16577, f.13v (*Italian Machzor*)
Word panel adorned with floral motifs and golden buds.

(p.9) BL MS. Or. 5024, f.11v (*Legal Decisions*)
Foliage border painted in rich colors embellished with
gold dots.

(p.11) Bod. MS. Kennicott I f.352v (*Kennicott Bible*)
An example of the intricate and brilliant carpet pages, which
are a feature of this work.

**(pp.12, 16, 20–1, 23, 27, 32, 36, 42, 44–9, 52, 60, 63, 70)
Bod. MS. Laud. Or. 234, f.141v (*Catalan Maimonides*)**
Each of the markers alongside the section headings comes from
one or other of the various small panels with cross-hatching
and checkerboard features – stylized rose petals, stars of David
and other emblematic patterns – that form a quilted carpet page
dividing the sections of the work. The colors are rich; mostly
blues, magentas and pinks.

**(pp.12–13, 40–1, 58–9, 68–9) Bod. MS. Can. Or. 79, f.8v
(*Tur Even ha-Ezer and Tur Hoshen ha-Mishpat*)**
Border displaying various colorful birds (cormorant, parrot,
peacock) and interlacing tracery for foliage (decorative only
and not intrinsic to the text) in blue, pink and green.

(p.15) BL MS. Add. 11639, f.517v (*French Miscellany*)
This representation of the mythical bird *Bar-Yokhani* (cf. page
62), painted on a tooled background within a gold-framed
roundel, was probably modeled on drawings in contemporary
Latin bestiaries. Illustrations of the *Bar-Yokhani*, the
Leviathan and the *Behemoth* (the Wild Ox) feature mainly
in medieval Ashkenazi manuscripts of the thirteenth to
fifteenth centuries, and symbolize Jewish messianic
aspirations and traditions. According to talmudic sources,
these gigantic creatures will engage in a deadly battle and will
be consumed at the messianic banquet awaiting the virtuous
in the world to come.

(p.16) BL MS. Harley 5713, f.18r (*Liturgical Selections*)
A circumcision ceremony in a synagogue. The *sandak*
(godfather), wrapped in a prayer shawl, holds the infant, while
the *mohel* prepares to perform the ritual, watched over by a
small group of congregants, one of whom, in the center in bright
orange livery, could be the father. It is likely this scene was
inspired by decorated circumcision manuals and printed
editions of *Sefer Minhagim* (Book of Customs). It is an unusual
image featuring amusing elements such as the pointing gesture
and the dandified appearance of the father.

**(pp.18–19, 52–3, 62–3, 66–7) BL MS. Or. 5024, f.42v
(*Legal Decisions*)**
Multicolored border of intertwined leafy, floral and geometric
motifs, enhanced by a splendid red-crested blue cockerel and
gold dots.

(p.19) Bod. MS. Opp. 776, f.2r (*Liturgy*)
Two lions taken from an introductory panel in which the
animals support a canopy framing the word *Baruch* (Blessed).
This is the Jewish version of the crouching beasts that support

the columns of the ecclesiastical arch as an invocation of
prayer. In Jewish iconography, the lion represents Judah,
strength and sovereign power.

**(pp.20–1, 38–9, 41–2, 60–1) BL MS. Or. 5024, f.35v
(*Legal Decisions*)**
Dainty border combining floral and foliage designs strewn with
gold dots.

(p.22) BL MS. Harley 5713, f.4v (*Liturgical Selections*)
A cantor singing from a music score, wearing a long cloak and
black beret – the fashionable synagogue dress of the early
eighteenth century.

(p.25) BL MS. Or. 2884, f.5r (*Sister Haggadah*)
Episodes from Jacob's life. Above: Jacob arrives in Haran and
meets Rachel for the first time. Below: right, Jacob embraces
Rachel; left, Laban (Rachel's father) and Rachel entertain
Jacob. These scenes belong to an illuminated cycle depicting
events from *Genesis* and *Exodus*. Miniature cycles are a
common feature of fourteenth-century Spanish *Haggadot*.

(p.26) BL MS. Harley 5713, f.17v (*Liturgical Selections*)
The humor in this wedding scene rests in the bride's rather
casual demeanor (right hand on hip) under the ritual canopy.
The groom prepares to place the ring on the bride's finger while
reciting the betrothal formula. The party's attire, particularly the
groom's livery and cloak with ruff and the ladies' *fontanges*
(head-dresses), provide valuable examples of eighteenth-
century Western European Jewish costume.

**(p.29) BL MS. Add.27210, f.8v (detail)
(*The Golden Haggadah*)**
Lamenting Jacob's death. Gathered around Jacob's coffin are,
on the left, Pharaoh and four courtiers and, on the right, a
group of Canaanites dressed in dark hooded cloaks. This
miniature forms part of a biblical cycle placed before the
Haggadah text, and was executed by an illuminator well
acquainted with High Gothic artistry. This is manifest in the
mourners' expressive faces and gestures and their softly-draped
garments.

**(p.31) Bod. MS. Kennicott I, inside back cover (carpet
page) (*Kennicott Bible*)**
Another intricate stylized panel with interlacing tracery and
architectural forms.

(p.32) BL MS. Harley 5713, f.17r (*Liturgical Selections*)
Worshippers, in early eighteenth-century synagogual attire,
welcoming the new moon.

**(pp.33–5) Bod. MS. Laud Or. 321, f.89r&v, f.90r&v, f.91r
(*Ashkenazi Machzor*)**
Standard astrological signs signifying the months of the year.
The manuscript itself gives them starting with *Nisan* (Aries), the
first month, whereas traditional ancient Jewish astrology gave
precedence to *Iyyar* (Taurus), the sign for Reuben, Jacob's
first-born.

(p.36–7) BL MS. Add. 11657, f.327r (Bible)
Border displaying colorful foliage emerging from a crane's beak.

(p.38) BL MS. Harley 5713, f.5v (Liturgical Selections)
Man, goblet in hand, reciting the Kiddush (the blessing over wine).

(p.41) BL MS. Harley 5713, f.4r (Liturgical Selections)
King David enthroned playing the harp. Episodes from King David's life, particularly his role as musician and psalmist, were popular topics in Hebrew and Latin medieval manuscript illuminations.

(p.43) BL MS. Or. 5024, f.78r (detail) (Legal Decisions)
A drolerie, an amusing device showing a youth inhabiting a leaf, blowing a ram's horn. Such devices are often found in ornamental borders of fourteenth-century Spanish Haggadot.

(p.45) BL MS. Or. 5024, f.70v (detail) (Legal Decisions)
Customs for Sukkot. Above: a sukkah, the traditional hut built of interwoven green branches where meals are taken during the festival. Below: a drolerie featuring a beast attached to a half-length man holding the customary lulav, the Four Species bouquet of palm, myrtle, willow and citron.

(p.46) BL MS. Or. 5024, f.19r (detail) (Legal Decisions)
Rites of Chanukah. A cloaked figure is lighting a Chanukiyah, the eight-branched menorah. The wall-backed type of oil lamp depicted here apparently originated in thirteenth-century Spain and would have been positioned outside the entrance to a house for the duration of the festival. The custom of placing the lamp outside went back to Mishnaic times and followed the Halakhic ruling to publicly declare the miracle of Chanukah.

(p.47) BL MS. Add. 11639, f.260v (French Miscellany)
Esther finding favor before King Ahasuerus, illustrating the verse 'Then the King held out to Esther the golden scepter ...' (Esther 8:4). This miniature was executed by an anonymous artist in the French Gothic style of the period. A characteristic feature of Gothic illuminations in Hebrew and Latin manuscripts is their checkered or diaper backgrounds, painted here in magenta and deep blue.

(p.48) Bod. MS. Laud. Or. 321, f.127v (Ashkenazi Machzor)
The figure at the center is shown taking matza from an oven; he is wearing a typical Jewish hat. The figure is flanked by a pair of lions (cf. page 19) or griffins, and a pair of bulls, representative of the legendary Behemoth, of eschatological significance because it is destined to serve as food for the righteous at the coming of the Messiah. In a decorative context these share the same attribute in Jewish iconography – power – and the two pairs are displayed with one head between them. The encircling horns of the bulls and the flourish of the lions' tails make satisfying images.

(p.49) BL MS. Add. 22413, f.71r (detail) (German Machzor)
Harvesting activities illustrating the story of Ruth read during Shavuot. Set under cusped arches, divided by blossoming trees and flanked by fortification towers, the miniature features on the right, Ruth, sickle in hand with reapers and gleaners; above them in gilded letters Va-yehi ('And it came to pass', the opening words of Ruth); on the left, threshers and winnowers. Some of the characters are portrayed with animal heads, an artistic device used in Hebrew manuscripts to avoid reproducing the human face, in response to anti-iconic Jewish attitudes in Germany in the 1320s.

(p.51) Bod. MS. Kennicott I, inside back cover (carpet page) (Kennicott Bible)
Another intricate stylized panel with interlacing tracery and architectural forms.

(p.55) BL MS. Harley 5686, f.60r (Italian Machzor)
Prayers for rain and the ravages of hail. The cloaked man kneeling under a sunny sky on the right of the miniature is praying for rain; on the left, two youths dressed in contemporary Italian attire look in awe at the orchard damaged by hail. Thérèse and Mendel Metzger maintain that medieval folk welcomed rain as a sign of divine mercy but were terrified of the catastrophic effect of hailstorms on crops and animals, and the ensuing famine and ruin.

(p.56) BL MS. Sloane 3173, f.34r (Leipnik Haggadah)
A portrayal of Jerusalem and the messianic Temple. The Holy City, rendered here as a thriving European town with beautiful spires and castles, is dwarfed by the monumental baroque Temple, its tower crowned by the Star of David. The sun rising in splendor above the city adds dignified serenity to the composition. As in other eighteenth-century Haggadah manuscripts, this illustration accompanies the hymn Adir Hu (Strong is He), expressing the centuries-long hope of restoring Jerusalem and its Temple.

(p.62) Bod. MS. Laud. Or. 321, f.308r (Ashkenazi Machzor)
The figure of the ziz (the messianic bird Bar-Yokhani, cf. page 15) without the accompanying egg that sometimes appears. One of the three eschatological beasts, the ziz shares the attributes of the phoenix and the griffin. It is rather plainly illustrated here and, like the lions on page 19, is drawn from an image where it stands as a supporter to a portal.

(p.65) BL MS. Add. 27210, f.4v (Golden Haggadah)
Jacob's dream in which angels climb a ladder, illustrating the verse 'And he dreamed; and, behold, a ladder set up on the earth, and the top of it reached to heaven ...' (Genesis 28:12).

(p.71) Bod. MS. Can. Or. 62, f.40v (detail) (Ashkenazi Pentateuch)
An elaborate image of a peacock and foliage, used as a lead for the beginning of a parashah.

Details of Bodleian Library manuscripts compiled by Stephen Massil, Hebraica Libraries Group.
Details of British Museum manuscripts compiled by Ilana Tahan, Curator of the Hebrew Section of the British Library.